POWSELS AND THRUMS

POWSELS AND THRUMS

A Tapestry of a Creative Life

Alan Garner

4th ESTATE · *London*

4th Estate
An imprint of HarperCollins*Publishers*
1 London Bridge Street
London SE1 9GF

www.4thestate.co.uk

HarperCollins*Publishers*
Macken House
39/40 Mayor Street Upper
Dublin 1
D01 C9W8, Ireland

First published in Great Britain in 2024 by 4th Estate

4

Edited by Robert Lacey

A catalogue record for this book is available from the British Library

ISBN 978-0-00-872521-1

Typeset in Adobe Garamond Pro
by Palimpsest Book Production Ltd, Falkirk, Stirlingshire

Printed and bound in the UK using 100% renewable electricity at
CPI Group (UK) Ltd

This book contains FSC™ certified paper and other controlled sources
to ensure responsible forest management.

For more information visit: www.harpercollins.co.uk/green

In memoriam
Joseph Garner
1875–1955

Contents

Introduction

Joseph Garner was my grandfather. His great-grandfather Joseph was a Little Master, as was that Joseph's son William. They worked in a room at the end of the house, a room that even in my childhood was still called 'Uncle's'.

They were self-employed handloom weavers, and sold their woven lengths to Big Masters at Macclesfield and Stockport markets every week, walking both ways, and carrying back the next batch of raw thread to the loom.

Handloom weaving produced snippets of cloth which the weaver kept for his own use. These oddments were known as 'powsels and thrums'; and Joseph's and William's families would have been clad with the bits that skill had brought together to make something whole and new.

As with weaving, so with writing.

A lifetime of working with a pen produces pieces of thought, the powsels and thrums of research and experience and imagination and story, that stand alone but, because they are the product of the same loom, carry a common thread that can be shaped into something more than its parts.

And that is what is offered here.

Come here, lad, and I'll tell thee a tale.
I'll tell thee a tale about a weasel and a snail,
A monkey and a merry abbot,
Seven good sons for winding.

1

Damper Latham

Grandad was a triple smith; white, black and lock. His best friend was Damper Latham, a living-in servant at Croston Towers, one of the big houses up Woodbrook Road on the Back Hill. One night, on Damper's evening off, they were drinking together in The Trafford Arms; and when it was last orders and closing time Damper said to Grandad, 'I'm feeling poorly, Joe. Will you see us home?'

'I will, Damper,' said Grandad. And they set off to the hill.

When they reached Croston Towers the house was shut up and the lights were out.

'What must I do, Joe?' said Damper. 'It's more than me job's worth to be found like this. I'll get the sack.'

'Don't thee fret, Damper,' said Grandad. 'I'll see thee right.' And they went round the house to look for a way in. But the doors and windows were locked.

'Here we are, Damper,' said Grandad. 'This'll do nicely.' He had found the grid to the coal cellar, and he lifted it off, sat Damper on the edge of the chute and pushed.

Damper disappeared and there was a clatter as he landed on the coals below.

'Is all well, Damper?' said Grandad.

'I think so, Joe,' said Damper in the dark.

'Then I must bid thee goodnight, Damper,' said Grandad, and he put the grid back on.

'Joe?'

'Yes, Damper?'

'Cellar's locked.'

'Then I can't help thee, Damper. I must bid thee goodnight.'

Grandad went to the front door of the house, took his skeleton keys out of his pocket, picked the lock, felt his way down to the cellar, picked that lock and let Damper out.

'Give us a hand to get upstairs, Joe,' said Damper. 'I'm not fit.'

'I'll not, Damper,' said Grandad. 'It wouldn't do for the likes of me to be found in a place such as this. I must bid thee goodnight.' And he left Damper in the coal hole, went out by the front door, locked it behind him, and down through the wood to his bed.

I have the keys.

2

Hephaestus

Hephaestus was the many-skilled lamed god of smiths and fire. Grandad was not lame, though he did have hammer toes ('And what else should I have?' he used to say. 'I'm a smith!'), but he had many skills – not least on the E-flat cornet, which he played in The Hough Temperance Silver Band, founded by his own grandad, a reputed master of the ophicleide, which played at The Hough Chapel on Sundays and then, as The Hough Fizzers, busked around the farms for beer money during the week.

Whenever I saw Grandad in the village wearing a flower in his buttonhole, a bowler hat, and a winged collar, I knew I mustn't speak to him, because he was working.

As well as being a smith and a musician, Grandad was a bookie's runner. He worked the east side of the main street. Glyn Ridgeway worked the other side, and was often in trouble with the police, but Grandad was never caught. He had a photographic memory and wrote nothing down. He took bets as he passed by, not pausing even to speak. This ability had come to him, my father said, after he had been kicked on the head by a horse he was shoeing.

Grandad remembered having used fifteen tons of iron to make thirty-three thousand six hundred shoes for eight thousand four hundred horses during the First World War.

And he shoed me once.

He had a set of lettered metal punches for stamping the names of farmers on milk churns. 'I must have come near on writing a book with these,' he said. At the start of the Second World War all schoolchildren had to have their names on every item of clothing, for identification in case of an air raid. I went with Grandad to his forge to have my clogs stamped. He stood back to back with me and lifted my foot and held it between his legs, as if I were a horse, took the punches and tapped the letters into the alderwood sole of the clog. He knew how to hit to make a clean mark. When I tried, all I did was dent the wood.

Grandad used his memory as a hobby, too.

In the days when The London General Omnibus Company issued timetables, Grandad subscribed to them and learnt the routes and their schedules. He went to London only once, but Grandma said it was like having her own private limousine, because Joe knew how all the buses were running and they saw London without having to wait for anything.

He was also knowledgeable from boyhood about the village sewers.

His grandad was a stone-cutter and had made and laid the drains leading from the houses to the main sewer. When they were finished, he tied a rope round the boy and sent him to crawl through to check that they were clear. 'If the youth can get through, then shit will,' he said.

When, more than half a century later, trouble developed with the sewage flow, and the drains frequently backed up, the Council discovered that there were no surviving plans for their layout; but Inky Gesink told the Council Surveyor, Charlie Watkins, that Joe Garner knew how they ran. 'What can a smith teach me about drains?' said Charlie Watkins.

Grandad sat at his forge and said nothing.

Eh dear, whatever do they learn thee?

3

'Dare to be Wise'

'Please, sir, who's Aude?'
  'Who's what?'
  'Aude, sir.'
  'Aude who?'
  'Her father Aude. The school motto. "*Sa père Aude*".'
  'You mean "*Sapere Aude*"?'
  'Yes, sir.'
  'It's not your manky French, laddie. It's Latin.'
  'Oh.'

I was sitting at the corner of the kitchen table, writing in my exercise book.

  'What's that you've got there?' said my father.

  'Homework.'

  'Home? Work? Don't you do enough at school?'

  'No.'

  He pulled the book round. 'So what's this?'

  '"*Agricola aratrum amat*". Latin. "The farmer loves the plough".'

'Does he? Tell that to Ozzie Leah!' My father put his cap on and went to the pub.

Hugh Oldham, Bishop of Exeter, founded The Manchester Grammar School (MGS) in 1515, expressly so that any boy, regardless of background, might attend, free of charge. I benefited from that, and, despite the later machinations of ideologues, the school remains true to the ideal and is working to be able to return completely to a modern form of Oldham's vision by 2050 through a bursary scheme that is already in place and functioning.

In 1946 I was one of two thousand boys to take the entrance examination for 180 places.

The Exam

We were told to start. I turned over the paper.

Scholarship and Entrance Examination, 1946
Part II
SECTION A

Read the following passage carefully:

Gracious Heaven! the truth flashed upon me in an instant. I was sitting in the frail car of a balloon, at least a mile above the earth, with a lunatic! The horrors of the situation, for a minute, seemed to deprive me of my own senses. A sudden freak of a distempered fancy, a transient fury, the slightest

14

struggle might send us both, at a moment's notice, into eternity! In the meantime, the maniac, still repeating his insane cry of 'higher, higher, higher,' divested himself, successively, of every remaining article of clothing, throwing each portion, as soon as taken off, to the winds. The inutility of remonstrance, or rather the probability of its producing fatal irritation, kept me silent during these operations; but judge of my terror when, having thrown his stockings overboard, I heard him say, 'We are not yet high enough by ten thousand miles – one of us must throw out the other.'

Continue the story in about fifty words, to show how you imagine it would end.

I can't remember exactly what I wrote – apart from the last three sentences.

'So I gripped the edge of the car and vaulted over the side to wake myself up. This was only a dream. But it wasn't.'

My first reaction on seeing the school was to be overwhelmed by it. It was the biggest building I had ever known. And to be at the youngest level of one thousand four hundred boys, some of them seven years older than I was, made me feel lost. Worse was the daily travelling: two trains and a tram and the city crowds, after a life as an only child who missed over half the primary school years through various illnesses, and knew only the isolation and general lack of movement in a time of war. It took me several terms to adjust, not helped by one of the coldest winters in memory and the Mancunian smog. But after I had overcome the shock of alienation I was able to embrace this new world where I no longer had to protect myself from playground aggression but was in the company of equals, where to question was not only encouraged but expected.

There were three kinds of teacher: the old, who had come out of retirement because of the war; the middle-aged, many of whom had seen action in the trenches of France or on the shores of Gallipoli a generation earlier; and the young returning now, impatient to make up for the lost years and to bring about the future.

It was one thing to hear about the Athenian Acropolis from a whitehaired scholar, and quite another to be taught by a man that, only a short time ago, had taken part in a commando attack up its steepest face; or to learn Latin grammar from a holder of the Distinguished Flying Cross, who, after leading a bombing raid on Hamburg, had jumped into the night over Holland from his burning aircraft when he saw he could not get his dead crew's bodies home, and had spent three years afterwards in Stalag Luft 3, yet, some days, could not keep order in the class but would sit with a white face and rigid neck tendons and stare at us, seeing something else.

This combination of differing individualistic talents produced a richness and variety that I did not meet again. And what they had in common was the pursuit of excellence and the fulfilment of each boy's differing needs. And that need to question, especially to question received opinion. Here is a sample of their kind.

'Ikey'

Isidore Tenen taught me History in the first year. He was a big man, calm, with a patient manner and gentle, mournful voice, whatever his mood, and a hangdog face to match.

We had written our first homework for him. He walked up and down the desk rows, returning what he had marked. When he reached me he stopped and spread the pages open before me.

'And where, dear boy,' he said in his sad voice, 'did we find such lucid and exquisite detail to arrive at this eloquent conclusion?'

'In my History book, sir,' I said.

'Ah, we found it in a book, did we?'

'Yes, sir. This one.'

'Then we can't argue with that. We don't have to think, if it's in a book. My word, it'll be in a newspaper next. The *Manchester Guardian*, no less, I shouldn't wonder. That puts it beyond all doubt. Oh dear.'

He picked up the textbook and walked across to the window. He opened the window, sighed, held the book in both hands, ripped it in two down the spine and threw it out of the window. Then he closed the window gently.

'Now look what you've made me do,' he said, still sad. 'I've ruined your book, and the school will have to pay for another one.' He went to a cupboard and took out a mint copy and put it on my desk. 'Never mind,' he said. 'More money for me.'

I looked at the cover. The title read: *A History of England from the Earliest Time to 1932*. And below it was the author's name: 'I. Tenen'. Ikey gave me a conspiratorial grin, patted my shoulder and went back to his chair.

'Bert'

Bertram Parnaby came to teach English in 1949, our third year, and we were the first lesson of his first day; and I was the first boy to enter the room.

He was sitting at his desk, wrapped in his gown, reading, and took no notice of me. He was tall and thin, and the most remarkable thing about him was his face. Every feature was exaggerated slightly, with an almost cartoon directness. He wore brown corduroy trousers and a green sports jacket, leather patches on the elbows.

The last boys were seated. He went on reading. We waited in silence. He went on reading. Then, the moment before a cough or a shuffle would have been inevitable, he snapped the book shut, stood up smartly, opened his big eyes wide and said, 'Right, you lot. Cop this.

> "Whan that Aprille with his shoures sote
> The droghte of Marche hath perced to the rote,
> And bathed every veyne in swich licour,
> Of which vertu engendred is the flour;
> Whan Zephirus eek with his swete breeth
> Inspired hath in every holt and heeth
> The tendre croppes, and the yonge sonne
> Hath in the Ram his halfe cours y-ronne,

And smale fowles maken melodye,
That slepen al the night with open yë
(So priketh hem nature in hir corages):
Than longen folk to goon on pilgrimages."

'Get it?'

He had an actor's voice, resonant, clear, with northern tones. From that moment we were in his hand; and I had met one of the most passionate and compassionate human beings I have known, and a great teacher.

We spent the term being led through the music of Middle English by way of Chaucer and *Piers Plowman*, to the threshold of *Beowulf*, with Bert at the head, bearing our ignorance along with his charismatic energy and learning. Then, at the end, he gave us the homework job of adding an extra character to Chaucer and repeating it in the metre of Langland. I wrote this.

The Spyve

A wide boie ther was with us also
And seemed always to be in the knowe.
A spyve, in vesture straunge and loud y-dressed
His trousers, purple checkes, knife-edged pressed;
Greced down his lokes, his shoulders weren wide.
His neckerchief (O sight!) was alle his pride.
Alle grene and red and whyte it was, pardee,
And loude y-clashed the couleres, one, two, three.
His sokkes' hue outshone the yonge sonne
That hath in Aries halfe his course y-ronne.

A fag doun drooped upon his hair-edged lippe
While sold he nylons, rum (ten bob a nippe).
Ther nas no thynge that was to him a task
But it was there (ye do no questions ask).
Thys spyve of swynken had he no usage.
He flogged cars upon oure pilgrimage.

Þe Spyve

Þer slouching slovenly on the street corner
A felon was flogging chepe trashe he bore.
Nyluns for wenches and stockings of sede,
Perfumes from Paris Byrmyngham made.
He could get autos for export intended,
And egges from the farmer at twelve bob a doz.
Dressed he in garments worldly and wyked,
Shoen wiþ the crepe sole and toppes of suade;
A tye, a riȝt longe one blasphemous, gaudy.
His hair was alle oily and dreadful of siht.
And as he stood and leoned and took in some mugges
A watchman espied hem and moved hem on.

When Bert arrived at MGS he found a moribund post-war Dramatic Society; and he turned it into a force that attracted national notice and fed new talent into the Arts while enriching scholarship within the school.

Bert inspired love, and a part of that love was respect for his insistence on stage discipline. Being in one of his productions was no holiday from rigour. He was a perfectionist, and one of his rules was that we could not expect to begin to learn to act while we had a text in our hand, and the learning of lines was a priority. They might be edited during rehearsal, but we had to have the words in our heads, to be saturated in them, first. Tony Rubin learnt this the hard way.

In a production of *Bartholomew Fair* the day arrived when no book was allowed. The rehearsal was a crowd scene, and in it Tony had only a few lines, which he fluffed. There was a roar from the auditorium, and Bert jumped onto the stage waving a cricket stump, and chased Tony through the crowd shouting, 'I'll swing for you, Rubin! So help me, I'll swing!' We knew it was an act, but Tony ran, while we froze in our places until Bert calmed down.

This insistence on knowing the text saved me during a performance of *Hamlet* when, as Osric, I was left hanging by a technical fault, which I had to cover by improvising iambic pentameters until the fault was put right and I could return to the text. The audience did not notice, and Bert thanked me, but it was only because the text, and thereby the character, was so embedded in me that I didn't have to think.

Bert grew restless. Having built a reputation in the school he left to be a producer for BBC radio. But after two years he was back, frustrated by the bureaucracy, which he felt limited his creativity, and resumed his life at MGS until 1965. He then moved to Cambridge and joined the Inspectorate for Drama in schools and higher education, where he became Head.

By this time we had long been personal friends; and on an occasion when I was staying with him and his wife

Jane he said he'd done all he could in education and he was going to go it alone as an actor.

The result was a successful decade in television and film, after a period with The Royal Shakespeare Company.

Aged sixty-eight, right on cue, two days after Jane, Bert died.

'Heppy'

Hepple Mason was an English scholar. He never taught me; and we spoke once in my seven years at MGS. He was physically small, with a disproportionally high-domed forehead, and he walked at an extreme pace at all times, ignoring the world.

After the nuisance of the School Certificate examination, we entered the elite Classical VI, with three years ahead in which to hone our skills in the purities of Latin and Greek, unhindered by lesser matters, other than acquiring a reading ability in German, since a significant amount of classical textual criticism came from Germany. It was with surprise and disdain I saw that there were other subjects still left on the timetable, including English Literature. And my sense of its irrelevancy was confirmed when the first piece we were expected to take seriously was T. S. Eliot's *The Waste Land*.

I was confounded by the rubbish. Not only was it inept, pretentious and obscure, but it was shored up by notes of pseudo-scholarship, alleged to help the inferior and ignorant reader to appreciate the brilliance of the poem and the polymathy of the poet. This was not the suppleness of Greek or the compression and sonority of Latin. This was tripe.

A crisis arose when we were invited to react to the alleged poem by composing something that expressed our appreciation of its genius.

My first thought was to refuse. But that would be too negative and would leave me open to the charge of insensitivity. So I wrote a parody to expose the farce. It was published, without any consultation of my feelings, in the school magazine.

Mauldeth Road Station

Rain sliding stickily down the sky. Drizzle. Train in half-an-hour. Perhaps. Who cares? Nobody here, staff died years ago, all dead, ashes to ashes, dust to dust, corpses scratching behind dirty windows. Drip, drip, drip. Who lights the lamps? Always lit, never out, for ever and ever. Amen. Roof leaks. Walk along the platform, planks rotten; worms and fungus. Mind your step. Count one, two, three, four. Every day count the planks. Five, six, seven, eight. How many nails? Seven hundred and eighty-four planks, not counting level-crossing. Always the same, year in year out. Six nails for each plank. Rust. Everything rust, everything dead. Decayed. Ten past four says the clock. Always the same time. No spring. Perfect clock. Right twice a day. Lewis Carroll. Rain, rain go to Spain. Ten minutes left? Oh, God, let me live! Look up the line. Mist. Cold, damp. Souls of the departed dwell in mist. Odysseus dug a trench in Hell. Sheep's blood. Mist. The dead drinking. For the blood is the life. Scarlet mist! Wires quiver, the signal creaks. Life! All clear. *Introibo ad altare Dei.* Green eye of the little yellow god. *Qui laetificat iuventutem meam.* Who said that? The train is here; black hearse. *Nunc dimittis.*

Shortly after the appearance of my debunking of *The Waste Land* I met Heppy as he hurtled along a corridor. He grabbed my sleeve to stop himself and looked up at my extra height.

'You Garner?

'Yes, sir.'

'Read your piece. Genuine Eliotean overtones.'

And away.

Sixteen years later I happened to be in the school and on the same corridor. *The Owl Service* had recently won the Carnegie Medal and the *Guardian* Award. Heppy came whizzing towards me at his usual speed, and neither stopped nor paused, but as he passed he cried out, 'What did I tell you?'

'The Chief'

Schools don't produce creative artists. One can only see to it that one doesn't stifle them.

Eric James

My first view of Eric James was that of all: the slight figure that greeted us in the Lecture Theatre on our first day.

I was struck by the quality of his eyes, which remained for me the most subtle and daunting item in his armoury.

With them (I was to learn) he could inflect nuance and also quell a mob. They were eyes that could face fourteen hundred boys and make each boy feel that they were looking at only him.

At the end of that first week, The Chief, as the High Master is known, took an English lesson unannounced. He asked us to write our impressions of the school. I devoted my time to a rant about the size of the desks, and asked how, since they were already too small for me, I could hope to endure the effect of them on my physical growth.

Towards the end of the lesson, Eric James swept up my essay at random and leant against the window. He read the piece in silence, then looked at me, and launched into an analysis of the school's problems during the Second World War and an explanation of how, though my plaint had been long recognised, there were priorities, and I could well end up, as I did, having to accommodate my frame to the torture of wood and iron for the rest of my days there.

The important impression left with me was that an adult authority figure had taken me seriously and had addressed himself to a First Former as to an equal. It was a hint of the man.

In that same first term, I was standing one day with my arms open, moving them up and down in unison, on the steps leading to the out of bounds basement opposite the library.

A cold voice above me said, 'What are you doing?' It was a most sceptical Chief.

I said, 'Thinking, sir.'

'Good,' he said. 'About what?'

'Count Dracula, sir.'

'Forgive the intrusion,' he said; and went.

I wish The Chief could have met Grandad. They would have understood each other. Grandad had brought me up to observe two requirements of a fulfilled life. The first was: 'Always take as long as the job tells thee; because it'll be there when tha's not, and we don't want folk saying, "What fool made that codge?"' The second was: 'If the other feller can do it, let him.' That is: seek out within you that which is uniquely yours, and pursue it, regardless of cost. Eric James would have agreed.

About the least sought duty of a prefect was to read the Lesson each morning for a week. The choice of text was up to the individual, but on the Friday before our practice in public speaking, we each had to justify our selection in an interview with The Chief, a Fabian agnostic.

As my turn came, I was more than at a loss. So, in desperation, I solicited a member of one of the more evangelical groups at school, who happily supplied me with five extracts from The Book of Revelation, and I presented myself at the High Master's study.

The Chief heard me out. Then he said, 'Do you belong to a sect?'

'No, sir.'

'Then I suggest you spend the weekend in some other areas of the Bible,' he said. 'And let me have the list before nine o'clock on Monday.' As I closed the door, thoroughly rumbled, he said, 'Try 1 Corinthians 13, for a start, and see what you think.'

* * *

When, years later, after National Service and Oxford, writing happened, I met Eric James by coincidence as we occupied adjacent stalls in a urinal. 'What are you doing, besides the obvious?' he asked.

Now, it is possible to say, 'I have written.' It is possible to say, 'I have written, and failed.' It is not possible to say, 'I'm going to write.' The pretentious words cannot be spoken. Yet those eyes were on me; and they were blue in a way that I recognised. I said, 'I'm going to write.'

'Then write,' he said. 'I've always hoped I'd get one.'

4

Golden Mean

I wrote this for Robert Powell to read on the radio. Robert is the best reader of my work. We were both, ten years apart, fundamentally influenced by Bert Parnaby at MGS. When Robert was asked why he recorded so much of what I write he replied, 'I know where Alan's coming from.' And he does.

Listen.

First Love. It matters. It comes once. Never again. It doesn't repeat. It's not recurring. There's no dot over the decimal. I'll tell you. I've got to tell you.

Now then. Measure the length of your bank card and divide it by its breadth. The answer is one point six one eight. Now take a four-bar Kit-Kat. It must be the four. Measure it the same way. Answer: one point six one eight. And so are a lot of matchboxes. But not the Strike Anywhere the Original Cook's Matches, or Swan Vesta the Smoker's Match. I don't smoke. Smoking kills you. It says so on the packet.

It's the same with the planets. If you start with Mercury,

29

nearest the Sun, and call that 'One', then the difference of ratio between its orbit and that of Venus is one point six one eight – approximately. And so on; right the way out.

Big hospital doors are the same as bank cards. I mean big doors in hospitals; but it may be the same when the hospital's big, too.

The human body fits. Even the head and face.

Talking of faces: when I was nine years old, about seventy-nine thousand seven hundred and sixteen hours, give or take, my mum told me that I was never to have anything to do with Welsh girls. Their eyes were too close together. I asked her what was wrong with that. She said, 'Never you mind.' And I said, 'But everyone's got two eyes, close together.' She said I was cheeking her, and she smacked me with the sponge sole of my father's slipper. It hurt a lot. I didn't understand. I didn't understand words then. I didn't know about puns then. And I don't think she did.

That's why I like numbers. Numbers don't change. They're perfect. Well. Nearly.

One point six one eight. That's special: what's known as an Irrational Number. I like them best of all. Now I'll tell you about Irrational Numbers.

'An Irrational Number is any Real Number that is not a Rational Number. Almost all Irrational Numbers are Transcendental, and all Transcendental Numbers are Irrational. It can readily be shown that the Irrational Numbers are precisely those numbers whose expansion in any given base, such as decimal or binary, never ends and never enters a periodic pattern.' Right? It never ends, never reaches Infinity. It goes on for ever and does not repeat.

My favourite number is Phi. That's a Greek letter. It's not the same as others. It's also called the Golden Mean, aka Golden Ratio, aka Sacred Cut, aka Divine Portion; and it's 'the unique ratio such that the ratio of the whole to the larger portion is the same as the ratio of the larger portion to the smaller portion'. Isn't that beautiful? Doesn't it sound good? So elegant.

The Golden Mean was discovered by the Ancient Greeks. It was a pupil of Pythagoras who proved it: Hippasus of Metapontum. But Pythagoras couldn't accept that Irrational Numbers existed, so he had Hippasus drowned.

I nearly drowned once. My mum's brother – that's my uncle – he said he'd teach me to swim. So he took me to the swimming baths and up to the top of the chute at the deep end and pushed. I hit my head and the lifeguard had to save me and I went to hospital with concussion. I still can't swim.

Anyway, another time I was in hospital and I was being taken to theatre. Isn't it funny how one word can make such a difference? If you're going to 'the' theatre, you look forward to it; but if you're going to theatre – well.

I was lying on the trolley, in the foyer I suppose you'd call it, with my feet pointing towards the big door. The doctor said, 'Just a scratch.' (Now that's good psychology. When they say: 'Just a prick,' you know it's going to hurt, because it's invasive. Also, it sounds a bit rude. But 'a scratch' doesn't.) Then he told me to start counting. I got as far as one point six one eight zero three three nine eight, and the next thing I knew I was back in bed in the ward.

What's good about Irrational Numbers is they expand on and on for ever, free as a bird, nearer and nearer to the Truth, but never ending, never stopping, never dying. I wish we were like that. I'd like to be Irrational.

But I forgot. I'm telling you about First Love.

She was my uncle's wife's niece. She came from Wales for a holiday. And how we quarrelled! She said I didn't know about music and I said she didn't know about rocks. We wasted so much time.

Phi's a part of Time, too; but that's Quantum Physics. Better to leave it.

Then we went to the pictures at the Rex Cinema. The tickets were two shillings and three pence each, and the bus fare was tuppence ha'penny, both ways. We sat two rows from the front in a double seat, on the left. It was in the days before wide screens such as VistaVision, which had an aspect of one to one point six six, very close to Phi. The film was *The Glass Mountain*, starring Michael Denison and Dulcie Gray, with Tito Gobbi, of operatic fame. It was about a composer whose plane crashed on a mountain in Italy in World War II and who was saved by partisans. He fell in love with one of them and turned their story into an opera when the war was over. I'd never heard music like that. And we fell in love. It was so . . . innocent. She taught me a Welsh word: '*cariad*'. I couldn't eat; and she couldn't; and there were two days left before she went home. I saw her off on the 14.12 train, British Summer Time. Of course my mum knew. She said, 'Did you kiss her?' I felt sick.

And that was that.

Now let's talk about something more cheerful.

The Golden Mean has been discovered several times. It was described by two Indians called Gopala and Hemachandra in 1150, when they were trying to find the best way of packing bins; and in Europe Leonardo Pisano Bonacci (1170–1250), he studied it. Leonardo's better known by his nickname, Fibonacci. I don't know why he used his nickname, but he was one of the cleverest mathematicians of all time. He introduced decimals and Arabic numbers to the West, and think what a difference that must have made. Where do you suppose we'd be if we were still stuck with Roman numerals? I mean, imagine if, instead of trying to divide ninety-nine by twenty-seven, which is three point six recurring, you had to divide XCIX by XXVII. They must have been a strange lot, the Romans. Anyway, Fibonacci used his Golden Mean to describe the growth of an idealised (although biologically unrealistic) rabbit population; then he did the same for counting bees; but don't ask me why.

Artists and architects had discovered long since that, by using Phi, or the Golden Mean, they could create feelings of order and balance. It's in the Parthenon at Athens, and lots of other old buildings, like Notre Dame at Paris. It's as if our brains are hardwired to respond. There's something about it that makes us happier.

She died young.

Only the other day, I looked out her photograph and measured the bridge of her nose and the length of her eye. It was one to one point six one eight. So her eyes weren't too close together.

I don't know how you feel about death or religion; and I don't want to fall out with anybody; but if you believe something, there's no getting round it by rational argument. In my book, faith and proof are oil and water.

If you asked me personally, I'd say that I don't believe but I am religious. It's not what I'm against, but what I'm for. And I'm for uncertainty. As soon as you think you know, you're finished. You're brain-dead. You don't listen and you can't hear. If you're certain of anything, you shut the door on the possibility of discovery.

The best way of explaining what I'm saying is a story I read in a book once. It must have been Hindu.

One of the gods was sitting on top of the highest mountain in the world, and he was crying. Another god came up and asked him what the matter was and what were all those ants down there so excited about. He said: 'They're not ants, they're people. I was holding the Jewel of Absolute Wisdom; and I dropped it; and it fell into the world and smashed. Everyone down there has got a tiny splinter of it; but they each think they've got the whole and they're all running around and shouting and telling each other, but no one's listening.'

I can't put it better than that. I'm not saying it's historically true. It's a good metaphor, but it's true in the sense that it gives us a chance to begin to understand. But once you know, you become a wazzock (that's what we'd call them round here); and wazzocks, they won't be told. They don't know how to argue, and they don't want to. They've no imaginations and everything has to be the literal God's truth for them. They've got feet of clay, and they wouldn't recognise a metaphor if they trod on it. They're all the same, and the worst of the lot are the atheists. They must have their cake and the tuppence ha'penny. Atheism's just as much a faith as any other, except that it's more ignorant than most.

Now I seem to have talked myself into contradicting what I said at the start about numbers and how they don't let you down, implying that people and everything else do. But I'm not. I accept that even Phi may be a metaphor. What I'm trying to do is to show you why Irrational Numbers are the closest I know to Truth. You can follow an Irrational Number for eternity (though that's a dubious word to use), but you'll never be certain. You'll never quite get there. Which is as it should be. Just as the donkey must never catch the carrot. You'll be closer than if you didn't follow; but if you're a wazzock you can't even start. Clay feet wear out on decimals.

So when I saw her off on the train, and that felt pretty final, without what happened to her later, I was wrong.

Death has no part in the Golden Mean.

I think of my Phi 'cariad' returned to every form she may be in and ever was, flying outwards, free as a bird, free from the damnation of certainty, free in the timelessness, free in the one point six one eight zero three three nine eight eight seven four nine eight nine four eight four eight two zero four five eight six eight three four three six five six three eight one one seven seven two zero three zero nine one seven nine eight zero five seven six two eight six two one three five four four eight six two two seven zero five two six zero four six two eight one eight nine zero two four four nine seven zero seven two zero seven two zero four one eight nine three nine one one three seven four eight four seven five four zero eight eight zero seven five three eight six eight nine one seven five two one two six six three three eight six two

two two three five three six nine three one seven nine three
one eight zero zero six zero seven six six seven two six three
five four four three three three eight nine zero eight six five
nine five nine three nine five eight two nine zero five six
three eight three two two six six one three one nine nine
two eight two nine zero two six seven eight eight zero six
seven five two zero eight seven six six eight nine two five
zero one seven one one six nine six two zero seven zero three
two two two one zero four three two one six two six nine
five four eight six two six two nine six three one three six
one four four three eight one four nine seven five eight seven
one one zero zero one two two zero three four zero eight
zero five eight eight seven nine five four four five four seven
four nine two four six one eight five six nine five three six
four eight six four four four nine two four one zero four
four three two zero seven seven one three four four nine
four seven zero four nine five six five eight four six seven
eight eight five zero nine eight seven four three three nine
four four two two one two five four four eight seven seven
zero six six four seven eight zero nine one five eight eight
four six zero seven four nine nine eight eight seven one two
four zero zero seven six five two one seven zero five seven
five one seven nine eight eight three four one six six two
five six two four nine four zero seven five eight nine zero
six nine seven zero four zero zero zero two eight one two
one zero four two seven six two one seven seven one one
one seven seven seven eight zero five three one five three
one seven one four one zero one one seven zero four six six
six five nine nine one four six six nine seven nine eight seven
three one seven six one three five six zero zero six seven zero
eight seven four eight zero seven one zero . . .

36

5

Feel Free

I could no more write a short story than I could write a long novel. The form is the literary equivalent of netsuke and is beyond me. But in 1966 £50 was £50, and I was skint. So I accepted the commission, and I also had an idea that I thought might become something. I sat down, took pen and paper – and within an hour I knew the idea would never take off. It went nowhere. It was only an idea. Nothing more.

Then something happened. I remembered a story from a tattered copy of *Astounding Science Fiction* that I had wheedled from an American soldier in 1943 when I was eight. I couldn't recall the title or the plot, but it had had in it a looping of Time that had terrified me in its understated implications. So I stole that and made it my own, changing everything but a thumbprint, the immutable point of fear. The result was 'Feel Free'.

The story still stands up, but its main importance now may be the historical moment at which it was written and the context of its publication.

'Feel Free' had been commissioned for an anthology on

a children's list. There was no editorial objection to the plot, which has a sophisticated climax, but there was uproar at my use of accurate northern working-class contemporary dialogue.

Hitherto, fiction intended for young readers was written by middle-class authors and had middle-class urban protagonists, who commonly arrived on holiday in a rural setting and solved mysteries that had baffled the indigenous population. The children spoke 'correct' English, or boarding-school jargon, while the natives were restricted to quaint approximations of regional speech. My own first two novels, through ignorance and inexperience, followed the tradition, though they refused to infantilise emotion, or to be 'polite'; and that was new.

There was a reason for this, which I did not see at the time.

The 1944 Education Act, of which I was a product, allowed free education of all children to the level their intelligence and aptitude required. The Act produced a crisis in English literature, which is examined in the Japanese academic Haru Takiuchi's 2015 PhD thesis 'Scholarship Boys and Children's Books: Working-Class Writing for Children in Britain in the 1960s and 1970s'.

Haru Takiuchi found that the works by this newly emancipated generation often featured an untapped language and culture that provoked, with some exceptions, outrage and confusion among editors and critics.

My own editor, who was not involved in the fracas of 'Feel Free', wrote that there was a danger of over-emphasising the literary needs of working-class children because she believed that it was not necessary for 100 per cent of children to be readers of books, and that only the 'literate working-class children' were likely to be absorbed into middle-class life.

Such was the censorial role of most book editors in Britain until the 1970s, when the emancipated generation was old enough itself to become the arbiters. Also this period coincided with the arrival on the British editorial scene of such as Julia MacRae (Australian) and Linda Davis (American), who were untainted by the crippling culture.

But in 1966 I had to stand my ground alone. And so, although it was written with no socio-political agenda, 'Feel Free' exemplifies a period of cultural change, when working-class children were shown to have aesthetic sensibilities, and it is included here as a specimen of that change as much as for any value it may have as story.

Feel Free

The line of sight from Tosh's den to Brian went under the giant panda's belly, between the gilded coffin of Bak-en-Mut and the town stocks, through the Taj Mahal and over Lady Henrietta's dyed bodice. The first morning, when Brian had started his drawing, the Taj Mahal had blocked Tosh's view, but when Brian came back from his dinner three doors had been opened to give a clear run through, and whenever he looked Tosh's eye was on him.

Tosh kept to his den, where he brewed tea, unless he was on patrol. He patrolled every hour, on the hour, up one side, across the back and down the other side, which meant that he came upon Brian from behind. He said nothing the first day, but stood at ease, lifting his heels and lowering them: click, click, click; and he sucked his teeth. Then he patrolled back to his den. There were no visitors to the museum all day, all week.

'What are you on?' said Tosh halfway through the second afternoon.

'Eh up,' said Brian. 'It talks.'

'None of your lip,' said Tosh.

But on the third day Tosh patrolled with a mug of hot brown water thickened with condensed milk. 'Cupper tea,' he said.

Brian put down his drawing board. 'Thanks, Tosh.'

'Yer welcome.'

'How's trade?' said Brian.

'Average. For the season.'

'Been pretty quiet here, hasn't it?' said Brian. 'Since they built the Fun Park.'

'We have our regulars,' said Tosh. 'And our aberlutions is second to none.'

'It's Open Day up the Park,' said Brian. 'Anyone can go, free.'

'It's all kidology,' said Tosh. 'There's nowt free in this world.'

'There is today,' said Brian. 'I'm going, anyroad.'

'What are you on here?' said Tosh.

'It's my Project for school,' said Brian. 'Last term it was Compost. This term it's Pottery.'

'So what's all the malarkey?'

'I'm drawing this Greek dish, so I can make a copy.'

'What for?'

'Old Greek pottery's supposed to be the best.'

'Fancy it, do you?'

'I do,' said Brian. 'It's funny, is that. I seem to be quite knacky with it. I might go on and do evening classes.'

'I'm partial to a bit of art meself,' said Tosh. 'Not yon modern stuff, though: more traditional, like: flowers and that. It makes you think how much work they put in, them fellers. Same as him there.' Tosh pointed to the Egyptian coffin. 'Yon Back-any-Minute. The gold and stuff, all them little pictures. That wasn't done on piece-work. Eh? Not on piece-work.'

'Nor this dish, neither,' said Brian. 'It's why I'm having such a sweat over the drawing. Every line's perfect.'

'Ah,' said Tosh. 'They had all the time in them days. They had all the time there is. All the time in the world.'

The dish stood alone in its case, a typed label on the glass: 'Attic Krater, Black and Red Ware, 5th Century BC. Artist unknown. The scene depicts Charon, ferryman of the dead, conveying a soul across the River Acheron in the Underworld.'

At first Brian had thought the design was too stiff and formal. The old boatman Charon standing with his pole, and the dead man blank as any traveller. The waves curled in solid, regular spirals, and the rest was squares, crosses, leaf patterns without life. But as he drew Brian found a balance and a rhythm in the work. Nothing was there without a reason, its place in the design so fixed that to move it was to play a wrong note. All this Brian had found in two days from a painted dish in a glass case.

'Have you done, then?' said Tosh an hour later.

Brian sat with his hands in his pockets.

'No. Eh. Tosh. Let's have the case open. I must cop hold of that dish.'

'Not blooming likely,' said Tosh. 'It's more than me job's worth. There's no touching. You can see all you want from here.'

'Seeing's not enough,' said Brian. 'That's why this drawing isn't working. It's all on the flat. And that dish is curved. Pattern and shape are all part of it. You can't have one without the other. My drawing's same as sucking sweets with the wrapper on. I must hold it, feel it.'

'And what if you bust it?' said Tosh.

'I'd not bust it,' said Brian. 'I'd never. And if I did, it'd mend. Come on, Tosh. Be a pal.'

Tosh went to his den and came back with a bunch of keys. 'I know nowt about this,' he said. 'Think on.'

Brian lifted the dish and moved his fingers along the surface. 'That's it. That's it. That's it. Eh, Tosh. The chap as made this was a bloody marvel. It's perfect. It's like I don't know what. It's like – it's – heck, it's like flying.'

'Well, one thing's for sure,' said Tosh. 'Him as made yon: his head doesn't ache. It does not. How old is it?'

'A good two thousand year and more,' said Brian. 'Two thousand year. He sat and worked it out. All these here curves and lines and patterns and colours, see. And then he made it. He made it. Two thousand year. He made it. Heck. And it's come all this way. To me. My hands. So as I know what he's thinking. He's telling me. Two thousand—'

'Ay, his head doesn't ache any more, right enough,' said Tosh. 'And that's a fact.'

Brian turned the dish over to examine the base.

'It'd do for a cake stand, would that,' said Tosh. 'For Sundays.'

'Tosh!' Brian nearly dropped the dish. 'See at it! Here!'

On the base was a clear thumbprint, fired hard as the rest of the clay.

'There he is,' Brian whispered.

The change from the case to the outside air had put a mist on the surface of the dish, and Brian set his own hand against the fossilled print.

'Two thousand year, Tosh. That's nowt. Who is he?'

'No, he'll not have a headache.'

Brian stared. 'Cripes! Tosh! See at 'em! There's no difference! Prints! They're the same!'

'They're not,' said Tosh. 'No two people ever has identical tabs.'

'These are!'

'They can't be,' said Tosh. 'I went on a course down London when I was a constable.'

'But they are!'

'You might think so, but you'd be wrong. It's been proved as how every man, woman and child is born with different fingerprints from anyone else.'

'How's it been proved?' said Brian.

'Because the same prints has never turned up twice. Why, men have been hanged on the strength of it; and where would be the sense if it weren't true?'

'See for yourself,' said Brian.

Tosh put on his glasses. For a while he said nothing. He looked at the impression in the clay and at Brian's hand. Then, 'Ah, very good. Very close. I grant you that. But yon line across the other chap's thumb. That's a scar. You haven't got one.'

'A scar's something that happens! It's nowt to do with

what you're born with! If he hasn't gashed his thumb, they'd be the same!'

'But they're not, are they?' said Tosh. 'And it was a while back; so what's the odds?'

Brian finished his drawing early. He was taking Sandra to the Open Day at the Fun Fair. They met at the bus stop.

'Do you like me frock?' said Sandra.

'Yes.'

'Just "yes"?'

'It's grand,' said Brian.

'You never noticed,' said Sandra.

'I did.'

Sandra laughed. 'You never. What's up?'

'Sorry,' said Brian. 'I was thinking.'

A bus came and they got on.

'You know Tosh, the Head Parky, him as looks after the museum?' said Brian.

'He's me uncle's wife's cousin.'

'Was he ever a bobby?'

'He used to be a sergeant.'

Three stops later Sandra said, 'You're quiet.'

'Am I? Sorry.'

'What's to do, love? What's wrong?'

'Have you ever hidden summat to chance it being found again years and years later?' said Brian. 'Perhaps long after you're dead?'

'No.'

'I have. I was a great one for filling screwtop bottles with junk and then burying them. I put notes inside, and stories out of the newspaper; all sorts. You're talking to someone you'll never meet, never know, who's not even born; but if they find the bottle they'll know you. There's bits of you in the bottle, waiting all this while, in the dark, and as soon as bottle's opened time's nowt and—'

'You do get some ideas, Brian Walton.'

'It's a dish in the museum,' said Brian. 'I've been studying it. Drawing it. I thought it was a crummy old pot, but when I started to work it out I saw what was inside it.'

'What? Messages and stuff?'

'No. Better. This chap as made it, over two thousand year back, he knew nowt about me, but he fathomed how to fit the picture and the shape together. When you see at it you don't get how clever he was; but when you touch it, and try to draw it, you're with him of a sudden – same as if you're watching over his shoulder and he's talking to you, learning you, showing you. So when I do a pot next he'll be helping us. It'll be his pot as well as mine. And he's been dead more than two thousand year. What about that?'

'Fancy!' said Sandra.

The bus arrived at the Fun Fair. Sandra was about to step down from the platform when she tipped forward. Her eyes widened and she clutched at the rail.

'What's up?' said Brian.

'I've catched me shoe!'

The high heel had jammed between the ridges of the platform, and Sandra had to take her shoe off to get it free.

'Oh, it's scrawked!' she said. 'First time out, and all.'

'Hello! Hello! Hello!' said the loudspeakers. 'This is

Open Day, Friends! And it's free, free, free! Walk in! Have Fun!'

'Where shall we start?' said Brian.

'I don't know,' said Sandra. 'Let's see what there is.'

'Hello! Hello! Hello! This is Your Day, and Your Fair! The Fair With a Difference, Friends! Where Only You Matter! This is the Fair With Only One Rule – Feel Free! Feel Free, Friends!'

Brian and Sandra drove a boat on the Marine Lake, spun candy floss, danced to recordings.

'Hello! Hello! Hello! Feel Free, Friends! This is Your Lay-Say-Fair! A Totally New Concept in Family Fun! Where folk come to stay, play, make hay or relax in the laze-away-days you find only here at the Lay-Say-Fair! Yes! And it's All Free, Friends! This is Your Passport to Delight! Yes! Remember! Now!'

'Me feet are killing me,' said Sandra.

They sat on a bench in the Willow Pattern Garden. Brian stroked the head of a Chinese bronze dragon, from which music tinkled.

'There's no one else here,' said Sandra. 'Why's that?'

'We're early,' said Brian.

'Isn't it dreamy?' said Sandra. 'Better than that old park. These flowers and gardens; and the bees buzzing.'

'Hard luck on the bees,' said Brian. 'They'll be dead by morning.'

'Why?' said Sandra.

'Weedkiller,' said Brian. 'You couldn't keep the soil that clean, else.'

'How do you know?'

'I read about it last term in Rural Studies, when we

were doing Compost. There's a lot in soil. You may not think it, but there is.'

'Oh, we're off,' said Sandra.

'No. Look,' said Brian, and leant backwards to gather a handful of earth from a flowerbed. 'Soil isn't muck. It's – what the heck? Sandra! This here's plastic!'

Smooth granules rolled between his fingers.

'The whole flipping lot's plastic! Grass, flowers, and all!'

'It doesn't kill bees, then,' said Sandra.

'Bees!' said Brian. 'They're not daft.'

He climbed up a rockery. The bees were each mounted on a quivering hair spring, the buzzer plugged into a time switch.

'Hello! Hello! Hello!' said the bronze dragon. 'Lay-Say-Fair! The Fair with a Difference! Have you visited the Pleasureteria yet, Friends? The LSF Pleasureteria is the Only Do-it-Yourself Fun-Drome in existence! All the Fun of the Fair! Yes! Free! Now!'

'Let's have a stab at that, shall we?' said Brian.

They rode on the Big Wheel, the Dodgems, the Roller Coaster, the Dive Bomber, the Octopus. The rides were automatically controlled. Lights winked. Recorded voices gave instructions. Bells rang.

In the Pally-Palais Sandra battled with air jets from the floor, and clung to Brian on the Cake Walk. They laughed a lot.

'Well, I'm glad summat's cheered you up,' said Sandra. 'I thought it was going to be pots and muck all day.'

'What shall we go on now?' said Brian.

'There's the Tunnel of Love, if you're feeling romantic,' said Sandra.

'You never know till you try, do you?' said Brian.

They walked onto the stage beside the water channel. There was a gate across the channel with a notice: Passengers wait here. Pull handle for boat. Do not board boat until boat has stopped. Do not stand up in boat. Passengers must be seated when bell rings. No smoking.

'Feel free, friends,' said Brian.

Beyond the gate was a grotto of plaster stalactites and stalagmites, and the channel rushed among them to a black tunnel.

'Queer green there, isn't it?' said Sandra. 'Eerie.'

'Special paint,' said Brian. 'It shows up luminous in ultra-violet light.'

Brian pulled the handle and a boat came out of the darkness upstream. Its prow was shaped to fit a recess in the gate, which kept it steady.

'Passengers board now. Take your seats immediately. Passengers board now. Take your seats immediately. Do not stand.'

Brian climbed into the boat and turned to help Sandra. She put one foot on the seat, then twisted awkwardly.

'Hurry up,' said Brian.

'It's me heel again. Caught in the decking. Give us a hand.'

They began to laugh. Brian tried to lift Sandra into the boat but had nothing to brace himself against.

'Kick your shoe off.'

'I can't.'

They pushed and pulled. A bell rang. 'All passengers sit. Stand clear. Do not try to board. All passengers sit.'

The bell rang again, and the gate swung open.

Sandra was still laughing, but Brian felt the water take the boat, and he knew he could not hold it. Already he was being dragged off balance.

'Get back. You'll fall in. Get back.'

'I can't. I'm fast.'

'I'm going to shove you,' said Brian. 'Shove you. Ready? On three. One. Two. Three—'

He pushed Sandra as hard as he could, and she fell backwards onto the stage. He lurched in the boat and grabbed at the stern to save himself. For a moment the boat hung level with Sandra as she scrambled up, laughing.

'Enjoy yourself!' she shouted.

The boat bobbed away on the race, and Brian stood, looking. Now he was in the grotto, and Sandra was distant in another light.

'Sit down, Brian! Coo-ee! Have a nice trip, love! And if you can't be good, be careful!'

She was swinging away from him, a tiny figure lost among stalactites. He stood, looking, looking, and lifted his hand off the nail that had worked loose at the edge of the stern. He had not felt its sharpness, but now the gash throbbed across the ball of his thumb. The boat danced into the tunnel.

6

RIP

A girl in our village makes love in the churchyard.
She doesn't care who, but it must be the churchyard.
They say she prefers the old part to the new.
Green granite chippings, maybe,
Rankle. Worn slabs welcome.
And after, in her bedroom,
She sees the mirror's view
Of her shoulder embossed
In Loving Memory.

Anne, why do you do it, you've nine 'A' Levels?
Why not, Anne? If bones remember,
You'll bring them joy.
It's as good a place as any,
Close by nave, rood screen and chapel of ease,
Peal of the bells,
Bob Singles and Grandsire Doubles,
And when you half close your eyes,
The horned gargoyles choose.

But it has to happen.
Eh, Anne, tonight you were levelled.
William Jones, Late of This Parish,
Was cold beneath you,
His great-great-grandson
Warm above. And you rose,
Though your shoulder didn't show it,
In Glorious Expectation of the Life to Come.

7

The Friendliness of the Long-Distance Runner

In the early 1950s I was a serious athlete. They were the days before joggers clogged the highway, so it was unusual for me to see another runner when I was training. We fell into the habit of meeting up and pounding the miles together for company.

All I knew about him was that he was a mathematician at Manchester University. He was stocky, barrel-chested, with a high-pitched donnish voice and the aerodynamics of a brick. He was funny and witty and he talked endlessly, but I often understood very little of what he was saying, and it became clear that he ran partly in order to think. He seemed to be obsessed by the mathematics of biology, particularly the patterns on butterflies' wings and the distribution of a leopard's spots. It was exciting to be with him.

We had much in common: a love of paradox, a sense of the ridiculous, a taste for punning ('Do you know Debussy's "On Cooking the First Hero in Spring"?'), and we had both been traumatised by Walt Disney's *Snow*

White and the Seven Dwarfs, especially by the transform-ation of the Wicked Queen into the Witch. We used to go over the scene in detail, dwelling on the ambiguity of the apple in folklore, red on one side, green on the other, one side of which gave death.

Beyond that, I remember a single instance of conversa-tion about his work. He asked me whether, in my opinion as a classical linguist, artificial intelligence was possible. Could a machine be made to think? After a couple of miles of silence I said that, in my opinion, it could not. And that was that. He said no more.

In October 1952, the police ordered me not to associate with him, but would give no reason for this.

He killed himself on 7 June 1954. An ignorant and vulgar judge had given him the choice of a prison sentence or chemical castration when he pleaded guilty to 'gross indecency'; and I was overwhelmed by fury at the prurient, gloating humiliation imposed on my friend, and by a sense of guilt that I did not, could not, help him; which lasted for decades, and was made only worse when a relaxation of the Official Secrets Act revealed his genius and work. He was said to have shortened World War II by several years and saved uncountable lives.

He died of cyanide poisoning. By his body was an apple, partly eaten.

On 24 December 2013, under the royal prerogative of mercy, Alan Turing was pardoned.

8

The Power of Ten

Forwards to the power of ten to the Sun's end
And beyond that.
Backwards time lies bedded,
Stripped by the wind, made again,
And a new time to be
Stripped by the wind.
The rain grates mountains that were over
    Snowdon
That were under seas.
And beyond that.

All time folds on a single moment.
The one point of light is
Intolerable.

9

Concerning the Common Nature of All

Dear Mr. Alan Garner,

I am Kim Myung-hwan, head of Seoul National University Library. I am writing to discuss the return of the book you mentioned in your email message to Prof. Kim Ju-Won.

It was a great surprise to read your message, and I will be really happy if you can return the book to SNU Library.

We are planning a small exhibition for the Korean War in the library lobby, this year being the 70th anniversary of the outbreak of the War. If we receive your book before the end of May, we will provide a special space in the exhibition to show this old rare book and introduce your story of having kept this book for over half a century. It will be a wonderful gift for SNU community!

Thank you very much!

Remembering all the British soldiers who fought and sacrificed their lives in Korea seventy years ago,

Myung-hwan Kim.

Kim, Myung-hwan
Professor, Dept. of English
College of Humanities, Seoul National University
08826 Seoul, KOREA

In September 1955 I was a subaltern, aged twenty, stationed in London, a fortnight from the end of National Service. A sergeant-major, going through to his next posting, came to me with a story.

He told me how, in the first days of January 1951, he and his men were trying to retreat from Seoul and were under attack by Chinese forces. They had taken cover in a library, without food or water. The temperature was −40 degrees, and the only fuel for a fire to keep them alive was the furniture; and the books.

A chance came to break out, and they made a dash for it. In the chaos of gunfire and darkness the sergeant-major thought he was not going to survive; but if he did, he wanted to have something to show for the experience. He snatched up a book as he ran.

He did survive. And he had the book. But, four years later, it was a memory he wanted to forget.

He handed me the book and I opened the cover. The title page read: *De Ratione communi linguarum & literarū commentarius Theodori Bibliandri* ['Theodore Buchmann's Commentary Concerning the Common Nature of All

Languages and Letters']. It had been published in Zürich in 1548, and there was an inscription dated 1709 showing that it had once belonged to a Doctor Du Doüet. On the other side of the title page was a library stamp, which I could not decipher, and an accession number, 50690.

I said to the sergeant-major that he should have the book valued, because it could be worth a considerable sum of money, but he said he was not interested in the money. He wanted to be rid of the book, and if I would not take it he was going to throw it away. So I took it. He went. I did not know his name. I did not see him again.

A month later, free of the army, I began my studies of Latin, Greek, Philosophy and Ancient History at Oxford.

I showed the book to my tutor. He was interested; and he told me that Theodore Buchmann was a Swiss scholar of linguistics who had edited the first printed translation of the *Qur'ān* into Latin. He added that *De Ratione* must be a rare book and I should care for it. So I did.

The years passed. I became a writer. And one day in 1974 my editor visited me. With her was a Korean academic, then living in America. I showed him the book and asked how I could get it back to Seoul. He said that it would be safer with me, because he was not confident that Korea was stable enough to guarantee the book's survival. It had been lucky once, and he did not want it to be put at risk twice. He told me to hold on to it. So I did.

I am still writing. But though words may last, flesh does not. I had to secure the future of a book that I caught in a moment, a moment when it could have been destroyed by the hand that had saved it. I was not interested in selling the book; only in getting it into the proper hands. I sought advice from Rupert Powell, of Forum Auctions. He said that the book was indeed valuable, but 1974 was long in the past, and it should go home now.

It was as simple as that. A courier collected *De Ratione communi linguarum & literarū commentarius Theodori Bibliandri* from my remote house in a field in Cheshire, and thirty-two hours later it was in Seoul, in time to take its place, along with its story, in the National University Library's exhibition marking the seventieth anniversary of the outbreak of the Korean War.

Faith has been kept. Right has been done. I am content. But is this alone how we should see it? Can we ever claim to possess cultural objects? Or is it more that we are merely stewards passing through the lives and the stories of such things?

For example, what of Doctor Du Doüet in 1709? Who and where was he? How did *De Ratione* first come to Korea? Why did the sergeant-major pluck it in the dark? I was its guardian for sixty-five years. What next?

While we wonder, the book goes its way.

10

Maggoty's Wood

Maggoty's Wood is old.
Nothing grows.
Nobody knows.
Nothing goes.

Grandfathers wouldn't dare
At midnight. Fathers told
Of giggling; children scared
Silent to the centre, whooping out,
Could do it once, learning rain
And leaves, badgers, and to walk
Lanes after.

Maggoty's Wood is old,
And when the lanes are sold
And the houses ponder through,
It becomes an Unspoilt View.
Where grandfathers wouldn't,
And where fathers told,

And children could do once,
Is Woodend Close.
And nothing grows.

Beneath the playpen and
Beneath the bed,
Beneath the arrogant garden,
Nothing goes.
Nobody knows.

11

Up Them Fields and What Was Found There

I had ridden past the newly finished giant radio telescope at Jodrell Bank looming over the farms in its nest of scaffolding. There was a torn piece of hardboard in the hedge; and on it was daubed in whitewash: '17th Century cottage for sale.' Next to it was an iron wicket gate and a green lane, down through a wood, past marl pits, by a brook, and through a tunnel under the railway; and beyond that a field. I wheeled my bicycle into the valley.

There was no seventeenth-century cottage.

The brook had eaten into the field, and I could see a section of cobbles that were each bigger than my head, packed and layered. Nothing was on the surface of the field, but this had once been a road.

I began to climb. Things started to happen.

The ridge of a tin roof appeared, with three brick chimneys: one at each gable end, and the central one offset so that it was twice the distance from the right-hand stack than it was from the left. I stopped, knowing, but not believing, what I saw. I went on, and with every step the building rose up to reveal itself. By the time I reached the gate to the garden I could not avoid the evidence. What I was looking at wasn't a seventeenth-century cottage. It was a medieval timber frame of longhouse proportions. It should not be there. It should not have survived. And more: it had not been tarted up.

My mind, acknowledging the importance, registered 7.20 p.m., Friday (Good Friday), 19 April 1957.

I went round the end of the house.

There were two doors in an early brick rebuild of the weather side. The house had later been made into two dwellings. In the garden by the further door a tall, thin man was tending some wire cages. He looked up and pointed to the nearer door. I waved, and went to knock.

Footsteps answered on stairs and a man with sharp eyes and black hair appeared. And so I met Ted Pope.

It was his half of the house that was for sale. He was an ex-prisoner of war of the Japanese and had come, newly wed, from Manchester to find peace and isolation when the house was put on the market in 1949. After eight years, his wife could stand the peace and isolation no more; nor the dust, the muck, the oak timbers, the oil lamps, the well, the earth closet, nor the half-mile of mud track to the road. They were moving, at her insistence, to suburban Wilmslow.

Several would-be buyers had turned up, but Ted had refused them. He loved the place and he feared they might spoil it. Yet within twenty minutes of letting me in he said it was mine. I had not been looking to buy.

It was eight o'clock when I set off to ride down the

front track to the road and back to my parents' house in Alderley.

I got home as my father was about to leave for the evening. Every night, he would wash, shave, put on his suit and visit The Drum and Monkey, The Royal Oak, The Trafford Arms, and The Working Men's Union Club, in that order. He started at the furthest and ended at the nearest, two hundred yards from his bed.

My father was a man of few words.

'And what's up with you?' he said.

'I've seen the only place I can live.'

'And where's that, then?'

'Blackden.'

My father pursed his lips and breathed in. 'That's a way.' (It was six miles.) 'Is it for renting?'

'Buying.'

'How much?'

'£510.'

'How much have you got?'

'Eight and thruppence.'

My father put on his cap and left. He was back within the hour.

'How much did you say?'

'£510.'

'You've got it.'

He then revealed that since my birth he had been paying a penny a week for me to be a member of The Independent Order of Oddfellows. And he knew that the local Lodge Secretary would be propping up the bar at the Union Club. As my father told it, the conversation went as follows.

'Our Alan needs £510 for a house.'

'Then he'd best have it. And I'll have a pint of bitter.'

So there I was, with a 100 per cent mortgage, eight shillings and three pence, and no prospects. It took twelve years to pay off the £510.

Writing is my primary concern, but the house became a close second.

It is a hall-house. The hall-house as a style of living is a system that combines practicality with control. In its most simple form it is a rectangular structure divided into three rooms, or bays.

The entrance, used by everybody, is by two opposing doors to a passage that runs through the building. On one side is the service bay, or buttery, to which meals were brought from the kitchen, a building kept separate because of the fire risk. The buttery, and the room above it, also stored food and drink.

The middle bay is the hall proper. This is a single room, open to the roof, and was the centre of activities: an all-purpose space for the household, but with its own demarcations. In general, the further you were from the service end, the greater your importance. Along the far wall was a bench and in front of it stood the high table, usually on a platform, where the owner of the hall, his family and honoured guests ate. In the middle of the floor and close to the high table was an open fire, the smoke of which drifted out through the thatch and windows. There was no glass in the windows, but there were internal wooden shutters, against the weather.

Between the fire and the cross passage, at right angles

to the high table, were trestles for the less prestigious visitors and the rest of the household.

After a meal, the trestles were folded and stacked aside, leaving the hall as an open space for sleeping and for social uses or legal ones, such as a manorial court, where men would be asked for an explanation for having taken deer or timber.

The third bay formed the private rooms of the owner and his family. On the lower floor was the parlour, which was used mainly for sleeping. This was entered through a doorway at the end of the high table. Above the parlour was the great chamber, or solar, with access from a gallery in the hall, reached by a fixed ladder. Here the owner slept and entertained his closest friends and most favoured guests.

The hall-house system was a microcosm of medieval society. All entered the building by the same door; but once inside, where they worked, sat, ate and slept was determined by their rank and position.

And the hall itself controlled the order and was the hub because it was open to the roof, and so prevented traffic through the house at upper-floor level. No one could move unnoticed.

As the medieval way of life changed, so did houses. Windows were glazed. The one central hearth gave way to fireplaces and their chimneys. The service end and the parlour/great chamber end had their chimneys at the gable, and the hall chimney backed against the cross passage. It was this characteristic spacing of the stacks that had alerted me as the roofline appeared over the hill.

With change and the possibility of more comfort,

hall-houses were either demolished and replaced or modi-
fied or moved down the social scale. The open hall had
an upper floor inserted. In Blackden and elsewhere
dynastic land-grabbing marriages were arranged through
the centuries, and by 1880 the Baskerville Glegg family
of Withington effectively owned Blackden. The tenancies
were reorganised and the farmhouse that had been made
from the redundant hall became itself redundant, and
by being divided across the middle, was made into two
tied cottages.

So: I was living in the buttery, the cross passage, the
lower end of the hall and half of the inserted floor above;
while next door, that is in the upper end of the hall, the
parlour, the great chamber and the other half of the inserted
floor, lived Mrs Carter.

Betty Carter was born Elizabeth Bentley in 1885. In
the 1891 census she appears, aged six. There is a brother,
William, 'imbecile', aged sixteen. The head of the household is her mother, also Elizabeth, aged forty-two. In the
other tied cottage is the Thorley family.

Going back ten years to the 1881 census it becomes
obvious that the two halves of the medieval aristocratic
hall were being used to house two families to man the
signal box at the end of the garden.

There was John Thorley, forty-two, Railway Signalman,
in the buttery, together with his family, and in the parlour
and great chamber were John Bentley, thirty-two, Railway
Signalman, his wife, and his mother Martha, aged sixty-
nine. The children listed were: William, aged six, George,
aged one, and Edwin, aged seven months. But the census
misses out a tragedy that the parish registers record. In

1879, before George and Edwin were born, William had two brothers, Alfred and Thomas. In February, all three boys were struck by measles, and Alfred and Thomas died. Mrs Carter told me that, with each death, her father prayed to God to spare him one. His prayer was answered. William survived. But his brain was damaged, and mentally he remained a child. When Elizabeth, Betty, Mrs Carter was born in 1885 she had only a sixteen-year-old infant brother, William, Billy. By 1891 the census shows that John Bentley and grandma Martha had died, and mother Elizabeth was alone with Betty and Billy.

The result was that Betty grew up to be responsible for Billy, and lived in the cottage until he died in 1957, two months after I arrived.

Billy was physically strong, but acquired no skills. Domestically, he scraped dishes, gathered sticks, pumped water and wheeled coal in a barrow from Goostrey station, a mile away. He was used as blunt muscle by the farmers around, never earning more than thruppence a day, and was the butt of cruel humour.

Such treatment angered Betty, but her survival depended on her employment by the same farmers, and all she could do was to protect Billy from exploitation where possible. I recorded this. 'One day I says to Billy, I says to him, "You're not going there again tomorrow." He says, "I am." I says, "You're not." He says, "I am." I says, "You're not." He says, "I am." So I think: Right, mester, right. And I hide his cap! But next morning, do you know, the beggar still goes. But when he comes back, he's got a cap! And I think: You can go again!'

Despite the isolation of the house, a wide social life was

possible. This was because the signal box was at the end of the garden. When visitors came, the signal was dropped, the train stopped, and the visitors got out. And they went back the same way.

Mrs Carter also used the railway as a clock. The midday train from Manchester to Crewe was called 'Noony'. By that and the sound of the bell of Goostrey church she set her day. She got up at dawn and went to bed at dusk, with the seasons.

Here I troubled her. Each Saturday I walked the mile to Mrs Smallwood's shop in Goostrey village to buy paraffin, with two one-gallon tins hanging from a milk yoke across my shoulders. Mrs Carter grumbled at me for sitting up at night, wasting money.

Mrs Carter knew her place. One day, she heard the Cheshire Hunt in full cry, and went out to look. The fox was coming straight for the garden, with the hunt behind. She shut the gate. The fox slipped past. Her ultimate landlord, hunt master John Baskerville Glegg, ordered her to open the gate. 'I says to him, "Mr Glegg, I pays my rent, and I pays my rates, this is my garden, and you conner come in."' And the fox was away, the hunt thwarted.

When Betty married she still looked after Billy, and her husband joined her. They had two children, Frank and Elizabeth. Frank was the tall thin man I saw tending the wire cages in 1957 when I arrived at my future. He was checking his mother's gooseberries.

Frank Carter was quiet, shy, gentle – one of the kindest and most modest people I've known. And he was and is respected as the most knowledgeable of all competition gooseberry growers. He won many prizes at the gooseberry shows, but his special gift lay in the production of new cultivars: seventeen in all. Most of the winning berries each year in the shows around are his. The genius of Frank Carter lives on.

Of course, in the seven weeks after moving to Blackden, before the annual show, I knew nothing of this, and my first real encounter with Frank made me wonder what corner of the world I was in.

I was walking home in the late-evening summer light across the fields on the other side of the railway, and I saw Frank Carter coming towards me at a slow pace, not in a straight line but wandering. He had crossed the railway by the stile that was there in those days and to which I was going. We were converging in an empty field, yet Frank showed no sign of being aware of me. Instead he wavered in his stride, sometimes taking steps backwards. And he wasn't looking where he was going. His head was tilted up and to one side, his eyes fixed and unblinking.

We were about to pass within feet of each other, yet still he ignored me.

I said, 'Hello, Mr Carter.' He answered, 'Hello,' his head and eyes not moving.

'What are you doing?' I said.

'Following a wasp.'

When I became less ignorant of the gooseberry art I understood that in the last weeks before the show, wasps are the great enemy. Frank had gone to watch his mother's berries towards sunset when the wasps were heading for their nests. He had spotted a dozy wasp and was tracking it, over the railway and across the fields; and when he saw it go into its nest in a hedge bank he took out the tin he had in his pocket, opened it, and tipped a lump of cyanide into the entrance so that every wasp would have to touch it on the way in and out. The following evening he went back to the dead nest, retrieved the cyanide and looked for another wasp to follow.

The naming of a new berry, when it has proved itself to be worthy, is a matter of concern. Frank liked to link to an historical event, so we have a 'Prince Charles'; or to a local name with which he had connections: 'Firbob' for Blackden Firs where Frank lived all his married life; 'Bank View' where his son Doug lives; 'Blackden Gem'.

Frank said that, although he produced the cultivars, Doug was the better grower.

My parents played a part in the naming of one of Frank's cultivars.

Frank wanted to commemorate his mother. My father suggested 'Betty Carter'. Frank's modesty shied away from this. He couldn't have a reference to his own name. So my mother said, 'Why not just "Betty"?' Frank was happy with that; but he had misheard my mother. And that's how one of the most consistent performers in the show berries was named 'Just Betty'.

But Betty Carter was not the only occupant of the divided hall. She was born there, and through long endurance, by 1949, was a sitting tenant, paying rent of half a crown a week. The buttery end had the more usual history.

Tied cottages could be vicious. They existed to put a roof over the head of a labourer and his family only for as long as he held his job at a particular farm. A family could be evicted, without alternative shelter, at a week's notice. I knew two families from that period that had lived in the cottage that Ted Pope bought and then sold to me. One of them, the Halls, had been evicted twice.

And here was the first clue to the special quality of the place, a quality that every occupant and visitor has responded to in their own way. On paper there is a history of rural poverty and insecurity, yet all have said, in their own words, what Frances Hall said to me: 'We never had such grand times as we did up them fields.' And that is how people react to this day.

Billy died. Mrs Carter was free for the first time in her life. Frank was troubled. He wanted his mother to move, to live with him. She didn't want to leave. But Frank felt a duty to look after his mother in his own house, half a mile away at the end of the track. Mrs Carter was desolate, but she went. However, she insisted that her furniture stayed with me; and she inducted me into the ways of the house.

Her main concern was the stairs. She said, 'They're a devil for coffins. You must upend 'em, and bump 'em.' She also told me about the treasure of the mantelpiece. It was of a beetle-ridden soft pine. The mantelpiece, said Mrs Carter, was so rotten and loose that 'many a sixpence' had fallen down the back. And one day, when my total capital bottomed at tuppence ha'penny, I took down the dust of wood. I found a seventeenth-century fireplace, three ha'pennies and one farthing, and several rusty steel knitting needles.

As soon as Mrs Carter went to live with Frank, Congleton Borough Council sent out the Sanitary Man. (This was in the days of accurate job descriptions.) He declared the cottage unfit for human habitation and imposed a Closing Order on it. I privily countered by moving to have the building listed. The result was Grade II*, the second highest.

The Sanitary Man was friendly; and when I explained the importance of the house and my intention to save all of it, he said that he would rather have one problem family here than two, and asked whether I knew a builder that could write a damning report. My uncle Donald was just such a one. He not only wrote a formal report on the state of the cottage and an estimate of the cost of making it habitable, but he included a confidential letter stating that, in his professional opinion, the structure was beyond repair and the only practical solution was demolition. The Sanitary Man sent both documents to the absentee owner, who lived in a mobile home in Abergele.

She panicked, and her father arrived to try to get me to buy the hovel. And here I entered on the biggest bluff of my life.

When the father appeared I created the impression that I considered him to be out of his mind to think that I would give the matter of buying even a moment's thought. The bluff was helped by the stench of one hundred day-old chicks I had installed in the great chamber.

In the end we agreed £150, which I had not got.

So there I was, lord of the land at last, with half a house I could not use and a tin roof over all, which needed buckets and bowls beneath in times of heavy rain where holes in the tin corresponded with holes in the thatch beneath.

Since first entering I have asked questions of the house

and site. Every question answered has provoked at least two others. I'll focus on one of the more coherent aspects, the period beginning in about 1335, when the male line of William de Gostre failed, leaving two heiresses, Alice and Agnes, who are recorded as having each 'half the share of Blackden'. Agnes married Robert Kinsey of Blackden, and Alice married Thomas de Eaton, a younger son of the family that became the Grosvenors, the Dukes of Westminster. And it was in this house, or a predecessor, that Alice and Thomas lived.

The de Gostre family had almost failed on one occasion before then, when the second generation lost its main heir in a mysterious way.

Thomas de Gostre died in about 1300 after '[he married] against his fathers will and his own worshippe, and through evil councell he did suche things for quiche he was done to deathe, for yt was shame and griefe to his fader and his frendes'. His younger brother, William, inherited, and his niece, Alice the heiress, married Thomas de Eaton; but again there was a mystery, and this time the family was lucky to survive. Thomas and Alice had six sons, one of whom was also a William, which should have been plenty, but it's recorded that on 1 November 1385, 'five brothers of the said William [de Eaton] were slain at Gosetre, and were buried in the chapel there'.

Following backwards through wills and probate inventories of the tenant farmers, the same building appears and is described again and again, until we reach the last two wills and inventories of the Eatons in the seventeenth century, when the male line failed in 1664 and the heiress was snaffled by John Kinsey, so reuniting the two 'shares of Blackden', after three hundred years, until by the same means Kinsey was outflanked by Baskerville Glegg, who sold off piecemeal in the twentieth century, enabling Ted Pope in 1949 to get his foot in the door.

In 1958 the Merseyside and North Wales Electricity Board arrived.

The coming of the electricity poles caused a shock. From the small spoil heap at the foot of one of the poles by the garden the rain washed out a Mesolithic flint implement that had been shaped eight thousand years earlier. Once recognised, we began to see them: Mesolithic, Neolithic, Bronze Age: a span of seven thousand years.

Subsequent maintenance works have shown that the house probably stands on a prehistoric burial mound, where we disturbed a cremation, which has been radiocarbon dated, with 90 per cent probability, to 1830 BC.

In the urn fragments was a mixture of charcoal and what looked like broken dog biscuits, which, when analysed, turned out to be human incisor roots, representing more than one body, and various other human bones and a tooth of a pig or wild boar.

But the site has been occupied for even longer, since the end of the latest Ice Age, which was ten thousand years ago.

The earliest evidence of occupation are Mesolithic microliths, both implements and, more importantly, the waste from their making; which shows that here is where the tools were made.

For ten thousand years people have found here a good place to live. And not only that. It had been used as a sacred site for millennia. Over the years, in a damp corner of the garden, which is a silted-up spring, an Early Bronze Age axe head, an Iron Age copper alloy bowl and a fourth-century Roman coin, minted in Antioch, have emerged from the soil. What else may be there we do not know, because the area will not be touched unless a full archaeological excavation can be carried out.

By 1968 this good place to live was becoming stressed by a growing family and library. We knew our responsibilities to the building and the site. But we were expanding, and ideally, in the twentieth century, needed two more rooms, and a lavatory, and a bathroom and a septic tank.

A writer has no predictable income, and has to budget on what is in the bank already, not on the future. We were used to that. So when *The Owl Service* was adapted for television, we had an unbudgeted windfall: enough to fulfil our needs. But an old house is sensitive, and a timber frame is more sensitive still. You have to listen to it. It will tell you what to do.

It took a year to find the right architect, a young man, Michael Peach, who lived in Malvern. My wife, Griselda, sent him a detailed sketch of the timber frame, and he came to look for himself because he thought that Griselda couldn't draw. When he saw that she could, he became so excited that he offered to do a complete survey, which took him a week; and each night over supper he revealed the wonders he had found.

We were carried away by his verification of what we had sensed. But on the evening before his final day I had to remind him of what we needed: two more rooms, and a lavatory, and a bathroom and a septic tank.

Michael was not at all fazed. He said that the traditional way to enlarge a house in the days of timber framing was to add a bay, or bays, and that often this was done by recycling parts of other buildings. He then revealed that he had been involved in a *cause célèbre* on behalf of a forerunner of English Heritage in a battle to preserve from demolition a listed building that scholars of the time argued was the finest surviving and only known complete domestic Tudor timber frame. The opposition was the Ministry of Transport, which said that the building was on a dangerous bend of a main road that had to be widened. After four years, the Ministry of Transport had prevailed and the house, known as The Medicine House, was going to be demolished the next week.

Michael said that we should go to look at The Medicine House, which was eighteen miles away, at Wrinehill, now in Staffordshire but originally in Cheshire. And if we liked any of it we should take as much as we wanted, Michael would find a way of joining the pieces to our building, and that would be the solution to our needs.

We went.

The structure was so beautiful that we could not turn away.

There was a brick cladding over most of the external timbers. Inside was a wonder, covered by centuries of wallpaper, plaster and gunge. To take only a part of it would have been to connive at vandalism. So we decided to take the lot, ten rooms in all. And since we could not possibly afford that, there was no point in dithering. We bought the house. It cost £1.

A gifted carpenter was to hand and, with Michael's planning, the timber frame was dismantled by four men and one apprentice, using only block and tackle, every timber numbered, and taken to Blackden in nine working days.

The necessary repairs were made, and then the process was reversed.

A timber frame building uses almost entirely a simple pegged mortise and tenon jointing system. Which is a logical procedure, provided the builder does things in a logical sequence; otherwise it's spillikins. The Medicine House was re-erected over eighteen months.

I was a climbing cameraman, taking more than four thousand photographs, and a friend filmed professionally more than five hours of archive.

The result was such a fine building that we couldn't put a lavatory and bathroom into it.

For them Michael designed a modern link between the two ancient buildings. And we continued our accustomed financial life of dancing on ice floes.

It remains to be said that the road at Wrinehill has not been widened and another house stands where The Medicine House was.

Now we had a prehistoric and a religious site, a rare medieval survivor and a Tudor masterpiece. And I had made a circular trap.

Having spent my adult life protecting the place against dilapidation and destructive 'improvement', here was now something so commercially valuable that it could not be kept in the family on my death. And the only people that would be able to afford it would be the very ones that would destroy.

There was an alternative; but it was worse.

Writers can kill their houses. What were homes and living entities descend into the aspic of museum culture, to visitor centre and collections of carefully arranged objects. This place was alive and loved. 'We never had such grand times as we did up them fields.' I didn't own here. No one can own ten thousand years. I was merely a steward.

'We never had such grand times as we did up them fields.' Frances Hall's words both haunted and saved me. This place was not mere archaeology and architecture. It was also a place of stories. And here are two that Frances gave me – along with a pair of wooden chairs surviving from her trousseau on first coming to Blackden in 1925, which she insisted should return here, along with their receipts.

'I'm going to see a friend one night in Lower Withington. So I put baby in the pram and hang a storm lantern on the front. We go down the field and up by the orchard. When I'm coming home and pushing pram up the hill I hit summat in the field. I pull back and try again. But it's no use, choose what I do. I can't see past the hood, so I go round and look. And there, lying in front of the pram, is a great brown bull. I grab baby and run to the railway and through the hedge and along the banking to the stile into the garden. Jack's sat reading his paper, and I say, "Barber's bull's in the field!"

'"Don't be daft," says Jack. "That bull's nowty and always kept up."

'"Well not tonight it inner," I say.

'"So where's pram and lamp?" says Jack.

'"I left 'em."

'"You barmpot," says Jack. And he gets a torch and goes out. He comes back with pram and storm lamp. "There's nowt there," he says. "You want to take more water with it."

'Next morning I go up to Barber's and I say, "John, your bull was out last night."

'"Oh no he wasn't, Mrs Hall. He's always kept up."

'"Well," I say, "he was in the field, and I banged into him."

'"Then it wasn't my bull, Mrs Hall. Else he'd have had you."

'But I swear there was a bull in that field that night, though I never did see it again.'

On the Halls' second eviction, after a row on a Saturday, they were woken the next morning by the farmer on his way to church shouting beneath their window.

'"You're out tomorrow, you buggers!" he says. And I says to him, "It's Sunday, and you mustn't swear. Go to church, like a good Christian."

'"Out! Out, you buggers! Get out!" he says.

'Well, there's no reasoning with that sort, is there? So I empties pisspot over him.'

Griselda and I could not let this richness, this home, be demeaned by the jargon of 'property'; or risk a Bronze Age burial ground being levelled to make a tennis court; or for the house to be turned, because of me, into a museum.

The place is alive, and loved. We had to remove it from the grubby market of the Cheshire Golden Triangle.

We did this by forming a Trust to protect the buildings and the land so that their vibrant life may be passed on to the future after our deaths.

And that's where we are. The Trust exists. Which makes me the last tied cottager of Blackden.

What goes around comes around.

12

The Carr

It's impossible to date the alder carr that stands below the house. It's mentioned in a deed of 1 August 1287, when it may have been used to supply charcoal for the fire in the open hall of the house, or, more likely, the house before it. The last time it had been cropped was in 1916, when travelling clog-makers camped in bothies by the brook and felled the trees for the men in the trenches of France. Since then, it had grown unkempt and was a dark acre invaded by other trees.

In the first year after I came to live here, I began to clear the fallen trunks and branches, carrying them on my shoulder. The next year I began.

The carr was nearly dead. If worked, it was everlasting, but now the stands of alder were too tall, too close. The underlife was choked. When I went into the bog I lost the world beyond. The stands were so thick that I could not see how far they reached. Although I knew the acre it felt to have no end, and the light gave me no direction and no time. The silence held ancient noise. Only by the patterns of lichen and moss, which were thickest on the north side of the bark, could I tell the way out.

The floor was leaves, black water and black mud, held by the surface roots that ran from the alder stools, the flat wide living base from which the stands grew. I had to place my feet with care and not linger. If I did, or if I misjudged a step, the crust would give and take my leg into the marsh. I had to pull myself free of the suck before the other leg was caught. When I rodded to prove the depth, I couldn't ground it. And it was not my weight alone I had to know. The crust told me what load of tree I might carry.

The ditch was effort. Coppices were shielded from the wild, and though the deer were gone, the ditch and bank that had kept them out remained. Each load had to be thrown over and picked up again. Then the climb up the field to the house.

The railway boundary was a relic line of ash, with hedges running from it to the brook, a corridor for predator and prey. Alder mixed with ash burnt hot.

I didn't take the oaks, but when fungus killed the elms I wore out a bowsaw blade to get three trees and snapped the helve of a sledge in their rending. And the grain in the wood could drop its branches with no sound. Old English had said it well. 'Ellum mon hateth; and waiteth.'

The bog was safest in frost, when the leaves were hard and stuck together. They let me carry two stone more. Snow was not safe. It blurred the feet to the feel of roots. And when the rain and February thaw came the crust was too wet to bear. Then, I left the coppice and went along the valley of the Common Dean where the alders thinned out, following the brook upstream by the old road through the tunnel under the railway, its arch curtained with a drape of ivy, to the marl pits of the carr.

Here the world was different. There was no guzzling bog, but a green causeway reclaimed by bramble; sycamore, hazel, ash, and strays seeded by birds, with space and light to grow; and celandine in season, and the wild garlic smell.

And on either side of the causeway lay the pools of the carr, eyes of black water dug to get marl, the lime-rich clay beneath the silt, to fetch life to the hungry sands of the field. The waters hid their depth and were mirrors for the trees and sky, their surface still in every wind, and each a trap.

The sides went down twenty feet and gave no hold, swallowing any weight they caught. I was wary. In childhood lore marl pits were bottomless. Here, once, a horse, a strong Shire, strayed and slipped; but its strength made it sink the faster in the ooze. Ropes and grapples could not get it out, and George Massey had shot it as its head went under.

I could lift heavier loads from the carr here, but it was further to the house; and after felling, trimming, cutting into lengths, I carried each hundredweight a quarter of a mile, along the causeway, through the tunnel, up the field and tipped it over the hedge into the yard.

Next, whether from the bog or from the pits, there was the cleaving.

Alder and ash were sweet. I set the steel wedge at the end of the cut, tapped with the sledge until it bit, then swung. The short lengths from the bog split in one go.

The lengths from the marl pits needed a second wedge to free the first, to ripple open the trunk.

A tree had to be quartered, and the quarter sawn to eighteen inches for the fire; then stacked into the house. An alder would last two weeks.

In the felling, elm could not be trusted to drop clean. The saw hit burrs and crossing grain, and jammed. The only way to free the twisted blade was to drive wedges in to ease the grip; and they too must be hammered sideways to get free. And all the time the elm might kill.

'Elm's cold as corpse-light,' Grandad had told me. 'It wants thorn to make it go.' And as I sweated I remembered his other wisdoms. 'Logs warm three times. Once to get; once to fettle; once to burn.'

To fell a tree, I first chose the line of fall, so that it did not snag in other branches. If it did, and lodged, the next tree must be dropped as well, and that was danger. A leaning trunk could not be governed.

I set my feet where the roots were thickest as they left the stool. I made a level cut low on the side where the tree should fall, and then began the main cut higher, sloping a little downward, on the other side.

The blade swished back and to. I went at the saw's rate, not hurrying, not pausing. The trunk sat quiet, and I watched the line of the teeth in the wood. When the line opened, I stopped and listened. If the tree was still I began again, but now softly, careful, listening, until the wood spoke. I stopped, listened; began again; the line opened to a thin mouth. I took the saw out, and listened; put it back and moved with gentleness, until I heard the tree grieve. I stood off; and the mouth gaped and the top of the tree

levered the weight so that it fell with grace, peeling the bark
to the small cut; and came free. A moment of silence then
the crash, and the floor quaked. A greater silence hushed
all sound. The white sap turned red as blood.

So I renewed the tamed wild, clearing from the centre;
and with the light each year growth came, and flowers
returned; and with the flowers life. A robin disputed the
saw.

For nearly half a century I worked the carr, until I was
nearer Grandad's years and the work rendered its account
to limbs and joints. The wild is coming back implacably.
Robin rules once more.

Fire on a wedge from a mis-hit sledge
Hammers the dusk of another day
In the yard hewing alder. The wood
That grew splits, telling years
Saw, cleave, and the spark dies in the air
Alder reddens to logs.

We were all the Sun.
Round and round the fire flies
For ever in veins, the long ropes of blood
Keep the same heat. And though it slept,
The spark waits
Somewhere between wits and the swung hammer
And the steel in the wood that grew
Memory promise or threat
We are the same waiting
In the dark yard.

Archaeologists came and excavated one of the Bronze Age barrows near the house, above the carr. With the burnt bone they found the turves that built the burial mound, and in them the pollen of the plants that had grown then: willow, hazel, ivy, ash; alder, lime, elm, pine and oak; moss, fern, bracken, heather, sedge and gorse; meadowsweet, vetch, daisy, buttercup; spelt, grass, corn spurrey, wheat; dandelion, chickweed and fat hen. Four thousand years ago all was fields, farms, ploughs, crops, cattle, order; an open world.

The dead men in the mound had tilled the same land.

13

Nova

A quarter of a million fires
Have breathed on this hearth;
The hearth in the house
Where the days have been
Hall and hut over the burnt dead.
The news is
A star flared in Cygnus.
I look.
So far away the star had died
Before the graves were born.

14

Lens and Land

The Focus of Being

Landscape spoke to me before I knew what it was, but I heard.

I must have been aged about four, and my father and I were walking along the rim of the scarp of Alderley Edge beside a sandstone ledge. We came to an embedded pebble of white quartz, and I asked him why it was there. 'Because it is,' he said. We were going to Castle Rock, a prow jutting above the plain three hundred feet below.

Some years after, we were standing on the Rock and looking out across the fields to the hills. 'Daddy,' I said, 'why does that road bend there?' 'So it can get round the corner,' he said.

My father was no fool, but we were seeing our same world differently. It was the start.

Later I could have told him that we were on a multi-faulted eroded horst at the Permo-Triassic horizon, looking out across post-glacial soils and the New Red Sandstone fault to the folded Upper Carboniferous Millstone Grits;

but he would not have been impressed. We read the truths in our own ways; and I was fortunate to have learnt both.

My family of craftsmen and labourers have inhabited, worked and served the same small Cheshire hillside since at least 1592, and their lives have been a part of its shaping. It is a universe on the scale of the human body, measured by paces; which is why I have not been able to encompass metric units. The land is the visible extension of ourselves, and we are a part of it. Here microcosm and macrocosm are one; and here the metric has no part, no poetry, no meaning. There is no unity of the body and the world.

Scansion aside, would Robert Frost have written this?

> But I have promises to keep,
> And kilometres to go before I sleep,
> And kilometres to go before I sleep.

A Welsh phrase describes what I am: *'dyn o'i filltir sgwâr'*, 'a man of his square mile'. For over six decades I have tried to translate feelings and thoughts through the mediation of landscape, the landscape that my family inhabited, worked and served and which enlarged and mirrored them; to serve in turn with words this piece of turf. The bond was more than metaphor.

It was symbiosis; and made intense for me by a childhood that was confined by sickness and war. People did not travel, and I travelled less because I spent nearly half the time in bed, ill, alone, unrubbed by school or siblings. The immediate surroundings were the whole of my world: the Edge, when I was well, and the bedroom when I was not. They were the source of stimulus and sensory education. The Edge gave me the texts of stone and tree and the grammar of earth and leaves; while the rough plaster of the room was a landscape for the mind.

All this expanded when I became an athlete in my teens. I entered a new dimension of space and time, where I was alone in a silence that was alive; alive with awareness, rhythm, oneness with something all-enfolding yet private, which no one else could interrupt. Training took me into open spaces, where legs and lungs could read the patterns of the ground. It took me from the unique Edge, away over the fields and into the hills. What I had scanned at Castle Rock I now explored, and, with one exception, everything I have written is from the land on which I ran. The symbiosis was complete.

One of my daughters has said, 'You're strange, Dad. I photograph people. But you photograph rocks.' She is right, and there is a cause.

The spark, the ideas, the emotions of a novel can come from anywhere. They do not have one source, but they convect and converge to a centre, a place that concentrates and expresses their essence; a place that I know. And in the physical particulars and the spirit of that place I find the distillation, which is the book.

Research leans towards making connections between facts; intuition is more subjective; and for both I use a camera lens, to sharpen me and to refine the essence. My imagination is visual. I see, look through the viewfinder, and, somehow, enter in. When I look through the viewfinder I am with the silence of the runner again.

I have always relied on a camera in working the land I know. A camera asks me questions. Why are you taking

this shot rather than another? Why is this one so important? How will you frame it? Why frame it that way rather
than another? What is the depth of focus? In itself the
question may be small, but each is a facet of bigger questions; and the big questions are asked before the age of
twenty. We need the rest of life in which to understand
them and, perhaps, answer a few.

So when I look through the viewfinder I am in no hurry.
It is a discipline embedded in me as the pebble in the
rock, but for a practical reason, which has resulted in my
not yet wanting to embrace the digital process. I always
use film because I always have. Film demands choice where
digital does not, because, from first beginnings, I have
known that when I release the shutter I am spending
money. Each shot must count. Cash concentrates the mind.

An ironic consequence of penny-pinching is that I have
a pictorial archive to which I seldom refer. It is as if, having
put so much effort into the experiencing, the choosing
and the recording, the print is in my head, and I do not
need to see a physical result. I have thought that I could
save myself more money by going through the motions
of photography without a film in the camera; but I am
not bold enough to take that risk.

Although the photograph informs the text, it does not
consciously dictate it. If I go back to a shot after the book
is finished I often say: Yes, that frame caught what I wrote.
But the energy has been reversed, so that the photograph
epitomises the writing, even though I know that the image
provoked the words.

What I record is unpredictable. I react to the moment.
I do not set out in search of a detail. I react to what is

there, whether it be panorama or macroscopic close-up; a vista or an emotion or an abstraction. I try never to impose 'me', but to respect 'it'. By the deed, the choice, I begin to see, and the effect is cumulative; it layers and shapes the story.

The detail, however, can be more than the moment. Sometimes I have closed in on a rock and known for the first time in two centuries the chisel and the blow. I meet my grandfather's and my great-great-grandfather's hands. When that happens, time collapses, and the distance is gone between us.

With the one exception, everywhere I have written can be seen from Alderley Edge, and therefore easily checked. That exception was the landscape of *The Owl Service*, which is set in and around the valley of Llanymawddwy, eighty miles from the room where I work. With the other books, questions of topography could be answered immediately. With *The Owl Service*, I could visit the location only twice a year. I covered the walls of my room with photographs to form a saturation of Welsh light and shade, so that Cheshire was obliterated and I was enclosed by three hundred and sixty degrees of Merioneth. At each visit I collected geological and botanical specimens so that I could touch and feel and smell. Ordnance Survey maps became a necessity.

And maps, too, are as important as film. They are a form of aerial photography, which lets me see where I am going and the palimpsest that has made the land. And because what I write is imaginative fiction rather than social realism, it is essential for me that the story is shaped and controlled by a physical reality within which the metaphysical is played out; otherwise the result would be arbitrary. Far from being restrictive, grid references guide the imagination.

I am not laying down rules, but describing one process by which a book may be brought into being. All writers know that the only way to write is in the way that they are able. My good fortune is that I have been able to live and function through a landscape where I can read a personal story and to which I have a duty, and which I have sought to translate from the personal to the universal.

Charges of parochialism, cramped-mindedness, obsession, humbug, could be laid against all I have tried to explain. If so, there is no answer.

> But I have promises to keep,
> And miles to go before I sleep,
> And miles to go before I sleep.

15

The Valley of the Demon

When I was an athlete I used to fartlek twice a week. This is a Swedish training method, which consists of alternating periods of faster and slower running, often over natural terrain, both level and hilly. I would take myself off to the southern Pennines, and there I would lope. On the afternoon of 19 July 1952, I was running across a moor at a height of about thirteen hundred feet. Ahead of me was a dry stone wall. On the other side was a deep lane.

I slid down the bank. My bottom passed over something smooth and hard. When I hit the lane I turned, and parted the grass.

A memorial stone was set into the bank: It read: 'Here John Turner was cast away in a heavy snowstorm in the night in or about the year 1755.'

The stone was weathered, but legible. I began to clear away the grit. I arrived at the inner corner, and felt for the rear. It should have been roughly dressed. Instead, the back had been as finely worked as the face. This was not only irrational, but would have added to the cost. It was, after all, no more than a hidden memorial in a lonely place. If it had merited such work, why was there imprecision about the date, 'in or about the year 1755'? I continued, turning my arm at an ever more awkward angle.

In the late of late afternoon, my arm jammed. I couldn't move. I became aware of the time, the distance, the isolation, the silence. I tried not to hyperventilate. At last, I found a direction of give. I worked my arm and was able to start to retract it. Then my fingers met a line in the surface of the stone. They 'read' the letter D. It was unweathered. It had not been exposed. Much later, having extricated my arm, cleared a space, and wound my hand back in, I'd traced what was carved on the hidden reverse: 'The print of a woman's shoe was found by his side in the snow were he lay dead.'

The hills took on a starker force. Though it was summer it was also dusk. The print of a woman's shoe. One foot set against that snow. Just the one. I have no means of checking, but I would assert that, if the distance from the stone to my bedroom could have been measured and my covering of that distance timed, the figures would still be in the record books.

That was the start. Not for four years after the epiphany at the stone did I come to see that my future lay in occupying a neglected splendour of a house and in writing there.

Nor can I say that John Turner consciously played any part. Yet throughout that period I was, from time to time, hunted and haunted by the moment in the hills. The print of a woman's shoe was in the snow where he lay dead.

In 1972, my closest friend was staying with us: Professor Ralph Elliott, of the Australian National University, and an authority on Early and Middle English. We had met after a correspondence initiated by Ralph as a result of his realising that we had each, separately and from different directions, arrived at the identification of the Green Chapel of *Sir Gawain and the Green Knight*. We were working with the 1:2,500 Ordnance Survey maps that include the *Gawain* landscape. Ralph said, 'Oh, Lord. Look.' He was pointing at the most desolate, remote, hemmed in by packed contours, bleakest farm of all, far from any track. By it was the word 'Thursbitch'. The elements are Old English *þyrs* and *bæch*: 'demon' 'valley'. 'Thursbitch' is first recorded in 1384, a time when names were descriptive only. This was no Romantic conceit. For the people of those hills in the fourteenth century that valley was frequented by a *þyrs*: a demon.

Westward of and below Thursbitch is the hamlet of Saltersford. The ridges that enclose and hide Thursbitch had been the extremes of my loping land of twenty years earlier. I had not been to the concealed valley, but now I saw where it lay in my physical and emotional geography. I had passed by its mouth on that afternoon, and now could see the route up out of Saltersford over the moor to John Turner and the print of a woman's shoe in the snow where he lay dead, three quarters of a mile from the valley of the demon.

Here I must say, and cannot explain, that in writing there are moments when things are brought, given and imposed. This was one such. It was laid upon me that the story of John Turner must be told. But I had no idea of what that story was or might be.

I wallow in research. The physical writing of a text is the cost of having arrived at it by wondrous paths, where so many apparently disparate ways are found to meet and intertwine. In this case, at the heart of the labyrinth, I found the Minotaur.

To begin, I went into the land of Saltersford. And because I am obliged to protect confidences, I must mention no names of the living.

My research led me to Enoch Mellor. I sought him at his home and was directed, in a blizzard, to find him. We met as silhouettes. Enoch was himself a Turner through the female line, and he said that the memorial stone had been erected by just such another collateral relative in the nineteenth century, but that the date was Christmas Eve 1735, not 1755.

From talking over a period of four years with Enoch Mellor and the people of Saltersford, a picture of John Turner emerged.

John Turner lived at Saltersford Hall, where his father was a tenant farmer. He was born in 1706 and became a packman, or jagger, with a train of four horses. His main occupation was from Chester and Northwich, carrying salt, to Derby, from where he would return with malt. His home in Saltersford was ideally placed on this prehistoric trade route.

On Christmas Eve 1735 (that is, when John was twenty-nine), he was on his way back from Northwich. It was snowing. But packmen were used to being on the road in all weathers and at all hours. They knew the hills better than anyone. They took no risks. Jaggers were essential to their communities and yet at the same time mistrusted. Travel in eighteenth-century England was not for ordinary folk. Most people did not move more than four miles from their birthplace in their entire lives. Jaggers were looked on as boundary-striders, as Grendel is described in *Beowulf*, wild men, *wodwose*, as in *Sir Gawain and the Green Knight*. They belonged more to the hills than to the valleys. Yet on that Christmas Eve, John Turner did not reach home. The next morning he was found dead, though his team of horses survived, covered by drifts. And by him, on the white, wind-smoothed land, was the single print of a woman's shoe in the snow.

That is the story of John Turner; and for the people of Saltersford it is a most certain history. But I was getting something else from those farmers. It was a sense that they were glad of my interest. They were, and still are, troubled in their souls by something they cannot describe and can only begin to articulate. And it is to do in part, but only in part, with John Turner. It is something compared with which the print of a woman's shoe is, figuratively, a footnote. And none of my informants is aware of the etymology of Thursbitch.

Their concern is linked to John Turner only inasmuch as John Turner died. Why he did is what the farmers wanted me to answer. I approached the research rationally. And the anomalies, which must always be pursued, piled up as deep as the drifts that had covered the horses.

John Turner was found half a mile from home. No jagger would die when he was so near. Let us assume that he had been overconfident when he set off up from the plain, where the weather could have been no more than sleet. Yet he would have known that sleet can trap, as I found during my research, when the weather closed in and I had to reverse a Land Rover for three miles in the low-ratio gearbox with differentials locked in order to get out of Saltersford, while in Macclesfield, five miles away, it was raining.

Even if John Turner had been overconfident, the jagger would have saved him. In order to have died at the point where he was found, two hundred yards earlier he passed through the farmyard of Buxter Stoops. The jagger would have known to stop if he and his beasts and their load were at risk. But John Turner did not. He died, and in the next century the event was marked in stone, with a message on the back that was not read until my hand did so in 1952.

Enoch Mellor was my most sensitive, yet most elliptical, informant. A straight question never brought a straight reply. His replies were clues for me to follow; and only when I came back with an answer would he deliver another. I was tested by an examiner who hoped that I should discover what had been lost; and I am not at all sure that his behaviour was conscious.

You must imagine stone houses dug into the hillsides. Wallpaper follows the contours of the masonry and then is moulded over the damp and unhewn outcropping of the rock into the room. After the first meeting with Enoch I always telephoned to make an appointment. He always agreed. The first time I arrived, his wife said he would be back shortly. He came into the kitchen by the one door from the yard, emptying the house of any residual heat. He turned on the only tap and washed his hands in the cold water. Then he did something I have seen no one else do before or since. He dried his hands by wiping them, back and front, on the hotplate of the Rayburn stove next to the tap. The droplets spat and danced over the steel. He sat at the table, and his wife gave him a mug of tea.

Enoch was welcoming, but without conversation. So, presuming that the initiative lay with me, I asked a question. He drained his mug and stood up. 'Well,' he said, 'I must be getting on.' He tightened his muffler, pulled his cap further down and opened the door. As he stepped into the yard, he said over his shoulder, 'What's wrong with this valley, Alan? What's wrong?' And closed the door.

I have described the incident because it is typical of the way in which Enoch Mellor and other farmers gave their knowledge. But their few words were pertinent beyond anything I could hope to get from a structured approach.

On another of my visits to the house, Enoch opened the door to go. He paused, and said, 'They never should have buried that baby in Thursbitch.' It was a quarter of a century before I realised how I misinterpreted an essential remark.

Despite Ralph's interest in Old English, the trail was leading me to the Turners of Saltersford Hall and to Jenkin Chapel.

Half a mile from the Hall is a meeting of seven tracks. It is first recorded in 1364, which is twenty years before Thursbitch, as Jankyncros, later Jenkin Cross: that is, 'the cross of little John'. A fair used to be held on 24 June, the Feast Day of St John the Baptist. And, until the eighteenth century, a monolith stood on the site. In about 1732, for unrecorded reasons, a cabal of Saltersford farmers, led by Richard Turner, John's father, built a structure on the other side of the lane from the stone. It is rational to think that the iconoclastic act committed against the monolith dates from this time.

They built their Jenkin Chapel. At first, it lacked both bell tower and chancel. The men knew how to build farms, not churches. There is even a domestic fireplace. But whom, or what, did they worship? The date stone is clear: 'St. John the Baptist June 24th. 1733'. Where the uncanny creeps in is that the Bishops of Chester, for sixty-one years, refused to consecrate, and then, eventually, only on condition that the dedication be changed to that of St John the Evangelist, whose Feast Day is on 27 December, half the year away.

St John the Baptist frequently accumulates folkloric and mythic and pre-Christian baggage. He is often mixed up with spirits of the wild, the man of the wood, the *wodwose*, and, in Southern Europe, even aspects of Dionysos. Is this why Chester refused to consecrate?

Walter Smith, a local historian, records in 1932: 'We do not know . . . what use the chapel was put to . . . we do not know whether any services were held there or not.' Even today, Jenkin Chapel is called 'the place where they marry the odd'.

Something else that was and is 'odd' is that, of all the Turners, John is the only one for whom there is no record other than the memorial stone. In the eighteenth century, and in the huge and empty parishes of east Cheshire, negative evidence proves little. However, in one respect, John Turner was different. He was a jagger. And all packmen had to be licensed. So the Church may have been slack in keeping its registers, but the Exchequer would not have been. Yet in the Public Record Office at

Kew there is no licence issued to any John Turner. The most important son of Saltersford, whom many claim as kin, is the least tangible, though his spirit informs the land. Enigmas on every side. A chapel dedicated to a headless John. The insistence that John Turner, who died when reason precluded it, died on Christmas Eve, the same turn of the year when, eight miles away, Gawain delivered his head to the mercy of the Green Knight, a *wodwose*.

I met Enoch by chance and stopped to greet him. He said, 'Well, Alan, what do you know?' (A conventional exchange.)

I replied, 'John Turner was not going home.'

'No, he wasn't,' said Enoch.

'He was going to Thursbitch,' I said.

Enoch smiled. 'Yes. He would be.' And he waved and was gone.

The modern map shows John Turner to have been on the modern approach to Saltersford. But the estate maps of the eighteenth and nineteenth centuries show something other. If John Turner had been on his way home to Saltersford Hall, he would have taken a left fork, now a footpath, but a road then, that drops straight to the Hall. He would not have diverged through the farmyard of Buxter Stoops, which would have led him either south into Macclesfield Forest, or up over Red Moor into Thursbitch. By the end of 1976, all roads, physical and emotional, were leading there.

By the middle of 1977 I could not face Thursbitch. What I was finding through research was more interlinked and unsafe than anything I could structure as a novelist.

I was not up to the job. Not until 1996, with the experience of having written *Strandloper* as support, did I feel less inadequate. I opened the files again for one last try, and set off for the valley again, with Griselda.

Before 1742, Thursbitch was waste. Then the high moors were enclosed. The track to the ruined farm follows the remains of the walls, passing through now empty gateways, of which only the stone posts tend to remain.

The gateposts of the southern Pennines are of a characteristic shape and size. But we came to a gateway where one of the stones was not a post. It was a monolith.

On the instant, the enclosures of 1742 were stripped from my eyes, and I saw the valley as John Turner knew it. The monoliths were coming in towards the ruin, which is by a ford. But when we got there, the house was irrelevant. Across the ford was the valley's heart: another monolith.

Its obvious phallic resemblance had been enhanced. The detail of the top leaves little to the imagination.

But most importantly, and verified by a stonemason from photographs, the detail has not been worked with metal. It has been pecked; that is, made with stone. It could be Neolithic.

We were now involved in something much older, of which John Turner may have been a part but was not the cause.

The field by the lane where the memorial stone was set is called 'Osbaldestane Croft'. 'Osbaldestane' is Old English, and means 'the stone of the bright god'. We found it inside the field. It had been respected by the 1742 builders, who had taken the wall around rather than incorporate it.

We began to use maps more intelligently. Beyond the ford in Thursbitch something catches the eye at once. The 1742 wall runs up to the watershed at the top of the valley in a straight line. It is a steep climb, and benchmarks occur with a precision of spacing that is unusual. And the Ordnance Survey does not place its benchmarks on objects that are easily moved. This regularity could be significant. So we crossed the ford and trudged along what was left of the wall.

There was a monolith at every point that the map indicated as a benchmark. Why were they aligned? I took compass readings. The stone row is currently eleven degrees thirty minutes East of North. I asked the computer, and it told me that in the Late Neolithic and the Early Bronze Age, the stone row would have pointed to the Pole Star of the time, Alpha Draconis, the Snake, who in Dionysian Greece was called 'the father to the Bull', as was the Bull 'the father to the Snake'.

I am no mathematician, nor am I skilled in the subject of archaeo-astronomy. A better brain than mine would be needed to verify or dismiss the significance of the observations. Yet the big stones remain an anomaly. They were brought and set up before the high places were enclosed, and that would have called for time and concerted effort. For some reason, they mattered.

We seem to be a long way from the print of a woman's shoe in the snow where John Turner lay dead; but we are not. It is all a part of the labyrinthine way of a novel, which gives the words on the page a depth for the novelist that the reader cannot, and should not, know. But, by some mysterious process, the charge is conveyed.

On the way down from the stone row, about a hundred and fifty yards from the farmhouse ruin, we came across a small, semi-circular marsh that ate into the hill from the brook, and at its inmost edge there was an arch of collapsed masonry.

Steps going down were just visible, and stone walls, but the whole was obscured and made dangerous by the broken roof slab. Nevertheless, with a torch, it is possible to glimpse a channel cut into rock, and clear running water. Why, then, with a well of fresh water so close, should the farmhouse have had an open flagstone tank to collect the brown run-off from the peat?

At high noon in high summer, Thursbitch is visually different from the first visit, when I didn't notice a solitary bump, an outcrop, on the horizon. Now I did. In the two-mile stretch of the valley, this outcrop is the only interruption of the peat ridge. We went to look.

It is an extraordinary feature, entirely geological: a natural recess, shelter and cave, above a confluence of waters at a ford.

The combination of a natural cave above a confluence of waters at a ford made sense. In my background reading I had discovered that such a place was the one most favoured by a *pyrs*.

Writers that draw primarily on the imagination rather than on observation have to be careful. A string of strange events soon becomes meaningless, unconvincing and of no interest, however brilliant the individual beads on the string may be. The paradox is that the imaginative writer is more strictly confined than is the social observer. I call it the 'What-if Corral'. I am allowed to construct the corral out of any materials I see to be relevant; but, once they are chosen, I am penned within the corral by the logic of the corral, which must not be broken.

By 1997 I had enough ideas to produce a 'What-if'. It came to me as I was looking into the fire. A Russian proverb asks as a question: 'What is lighter than silk, more lasting than salt? A story.' John Turner earned his living mainly from carrying salt, and the women of Saltersford earned theirs mainly by preparing silk thread to be spun in Macclesfield. The image of the Silk Road, the greatest trade route of all, appeared in the embers.

Of course, the Silk Road never reached Macclesfield. The Silk Road was not so much a motorway as a series of campfires along an East–West line across Asia and Europe. And every fire could be visited from the North and the South. Over the centuries, not only objects could be exchanged but ideas, stories, beliefs. And these ideas, stories and beliefs would have been in the mouths of traders, not philosophers and priests: a melting pot of the mind.

My 'What-if' was that fragments could have reached the southern Pennines and converged with that more than residual numen of the land, which held on to traditions that were not Christian and survived into the nineteenth century in that part of England. What if Saltersford were such a community? What if John Turner brought to it from his journeys complementary materials? What if his influence were still at work now? What if that were the reason for his modern but no longer understood import-ance to the valley and to the continued energies of the northern *pyrs*?

The 'What-if' frame was in place. Now the question was: what could the novelist plausibly do with it?

This novelist was also partly experienced in the field of archaeology, and was already asking questions of the big standing stones.

The more Griselda and I looked, the more we found. They all approximate, whatever their shape or size, to point seven of a ton in weight.

The Silk Museum at Macclesfield invited me to give a lecture of my own choosing. The possibility of working the evening to my advantage made me accept, and I floundered for an hour or so, bringing in mention of the John Turner memorial stone. Afterwards, there were questions, then the audience departed. I noticed that a man was hanging back. When no one else was left, he approached. He was late-middle-aged, neatly dressed and groomed; indeed, without deprecation, dapper. He said he had been relieved by what I had said about John Turner. He revealed that, from his qualifying as a GP in 1948 until his recent retirement, his practice had been the hill country to the north-east of Macclesfield. He had never been happy with Saltersford, and always dreaded (his word) a night call there. He said no more than that, and I did not pursue him, but I left Macclesfield convinced that this story was not historical and fantastical merely. So I directed my attention to living witnesses again.

One was the Anglican vicar responsible for Jenkin Chapel. I had first, and for the only time, approached him in 1973 for permission to have access to the key for the chapel. He was now retired.

In 1999, I telephoned the vicar. Despite the twenty-six-year gap, he remembered me. I told him that I now had a clearer picture of Saltersford and that there were some questions I should like to have his opinion on. I asked him for his thoughts on Thursbitch; and I am now quoting from my notes made during the conversation. He said that he had no personal experience of the place, because he had never been there. He said that, at his induction in 1972, his churchwardens had told him that it would not be safe for 'a man of the cloth' to enter the valley. One of them had said that he himself never went there, because it was 'not a healthy part'. The vicar followed the advice because he respected the men that had given it. He also said that the people of Saltersford think of it as 'no good place', 'not right', 'not safe'. He explained that this attitude was spiritual, and said, 'I wouldn't like to go up myself. I think the valley needs feeding.'

I wanted to put the phone down, but the vicar reported another incident. The people had told him that, in 1985, Thursbitch was filled with what they termed, and he did not question, 'a lot of electrical magic'.

Now it is one thing for a novelist to be intrigued by etymology, monoliths and anomalies and to draw on folk belief; but when, quite separately, a medical practitioner and a clergyman not only support but surpass the imagination, it is time to proceed with care. I needed to get back onto the land.

From an archaeological view, the only outcrop on the two-mile ridge was potentially significant in relation to the monoliths. It is geological and fixed. They are artefacts and placed.

It is possible to show that people in prehistory deployed

stones within a Western European landscape, and that they could have used them to make accurate lunar, solar and stellar observations; but, being prehistoric, they have left no record of their intentions. I put in the co-ordinates of the monoliths we'd found, and asked the computer. The valley of Saltersford, and particularly of Thursbitch, according to the computer, could, it seemed, have been used for over three millennia for the observation of stellar, lunar and solar phenomena. The constellations of Taurus and of Orion appear to have been especially plotted in the Neolithic and the Bronze Age. The system works on observations of rising and setting times at the fixed outcrop when viewed from the variously placed stones. Arbitrary points produce no results. I am not convinced by these observations, but I include them here for better minds to confirm or refute.

I went to see Mr X, a farmer born and reared at Saltersford Hall, the home of John Turner. I needed permission to drive along the western ridge of Thursbitch. He said that he wanted me down by dusk and he wanted me to let him know that I was down. I thought that Mr X had no high opinion of my ability to drive a Land Rover. But he continued. 'You see.' Pause. 'There isn't a farmer in all these hills around.' Pause. 'As will open his door after dark.' Pause. 'Not even to cross the yard.' Pause. 'Without he's got his gun.' 'Not that it would be of any use.' 'But it makes you feel better.' 'Somehow.'

With that blessing, Mr X sent me to cross his land. He had also given me important information. The masoned well of clear water in Thursbitch belonged to Saltersford Hall, and the occupants of the adjacent farmhouse had

had no access to it, and so were obliged to drink the muddy run-off from the peat. He remembered how, as a child, he had been sent from Saltersford Hall to place butter on a shelf in the well. The well's only purpose, he said, was to act as a refrigerator. That he had been made to climb more than two hundred feet and to walk over a mile to get to the fridge seemed not to be a matter for question. Yet it is still the custom in parts of Ireland for butter to be offered to sacred wells and springs in summer; and a frequent date for the ceremony is St John's Eve, 23 June.

Mr X also told me that the outcrop cave was called 'Thoon', that is, 'The Oven'. And as a final *coup de grâce*, he said that I should pass close to a stone with writing on it. So primed, Griselda and I drove up. We parked as instructed, and went to find the stone. It stands on a small platform high on the side of the valley. We could see it from a distance. The lettering, of course, we could not see at first, but when we reached the stone, its imperative, 'ORA [PRAY]', fitted our emotions.

Alas, the meaning is secular. The stone was used to mark the limit of the land taken in by Richard and Ann Oakes in the enclosure of 1742. Nevertheless, to come upon such a directive in such a place is an experience.

The many visits over the years had resulted in a change of perspective from that first *pyrs*-laden sight. Though always in command, the valley had shown varying moods, strong but not necessarily malign. It raised questions about the meaning of *pyrs*. I asked Ralph Elliott. His reply was: 'I'll be back.'

A month or so later, he sent his answer. *Pyrs*, he said,

is frequently a malevolent being. But, when it is checked in its every context, this definition does not always apply. He said that, if he had to give a single definition that would fit all occurrences, he would say that *pyrs* means 'something big'. It fits Thursbitch with precision.

The suggestion that was becoming a link between the anomalies, that Thursbitch evolved, millennia before the Silk Road, from at least the Neolithic, as a special place, a site taking different forms through different cultures, and the concept of *pyrs* as 'something big', made sense. Geologists and geographers, when they feel themselves to be among friends, will talk of the concept of a 'sentient landscape'. Since I am neither geologist nor geographer, I have no trouble over using the term. It describes my experience. And it showed me how I had misinterpreted Enoch's remark of a quarter of a century earlier.

In the hills it was common practice, carrying no social censure, to deal with stillbirths, infantile mortality, or the mishaps of inbreeding, by disposing of the young in remote places. When Enoch had said, 'They never should have buried that baby in Thursbitch,' his meaning had been: it was not in Thursbitch that they should have buried that baby. The offence was not against the child but against the place. It had been polluted. 'What's wrong with this valley, Alan? What's wrong?' Perhaps the secularisation of the monoliths.

The strongest aspect of the 'What-if Corral' was the consistent appearance of the Bull, in Thursbitch and in cults and religions through the lands of the Silk Road.

The icon of the Bull is the *ur*-Bull of proto-Indo-European myth, from which Western bull (and many other) cults ultimately descend, carrying with them variations on the initially strange ménage of bull, snake, the Fly Agaric fungus, the hare, the moon, ivy, honey and bee: all connected.

At last, my refining through a sieve of silk produced a novel, a fiction, that accounts for, and integrates, the anomalies, including the print of a woman's shoe. It is fiction, and I have saved the worst till last. It is an unresolved piece of research from 1999; but it is true, although if I had not photographed the evidence, both Griselda and I should have had to doubt our experience.

At the mouth of Thursbitch I noticed a block of sandstone. In it was fixed a steel ring. It resembled a bull-baiting stone; and I photographed it. We had collected the key to Jenkin Chapel from Mr Y. When we returned the key he asked, as usual, whether we had found anything interesting. I told him about the stone and said that it could be a rare survival, since bull baiting had been made illegal in 1835. Mr Y laughed, and said, 'Well, I suppose it must have taken a while for the news to reach these parts.'

Three weeks later, Griselda and I went back to Thursbitch.

There was no ring in the stone; nor was there any sign that one had ever existed. If it had been removed since our last visit, we should have found the remains of its seating, or at least a spalling of the surface. There was nothing. The surface was unbroken, evenly weathered and with undamaged lichen. I photographed it.

A particle physicist friend of ours, when he saw the photographs, pointed out that the iron ring was not rusted but clean and shiny. He said, without wonder, 'I think you experienced a time-slip.'

But the *pyrs*, if a bull, or even if John Turner, had the last laugh.

I told the County Archaeologist about the stone. He sent me a printout of the random finds for Saltersford. In 1985, the year of the vicar's report of 'a lot of electrical magic' in Thursbitch, a gang of men was clearing out a ditch not far from the stone, with or without a ring, and they uncovered a cache of bulls' and of aurochs' horns; and among them a Middle Bronze Age sword.

16

Jenkin

Moonrise to manset is a moment
Somewhere between.

It is not enough to enter
The bone of the mother,
The rope of blood.
It is not enough to enter
By hewn birth
The island of the strong door.

Four widows draw the plough
About the head,
And eastward the birches
Carry the riding drum
That beats for no travailing women,
Nor for soul's plunder,
But to find the man lost in the snow.

I shall not be older,
I shall not be younger,

Than I was in the beginning.
There will not come from my design
Fear or death.
I see not and I am not seen.
Where twilight and the black night move together
I gather all given and give back.
In the island of the strong door.
In the four-cornered castle.
In the spinning circle.
In the garth of glass.
Hinged on the sky.

A night to kill a king
Is this night.

Tha pisses more than tha drinks.

This lecture was given to The Manchester Grammar School Philosophical Society in 2002 and at Newnham College, Cambridge, in 2003.

17

Old Men's Trousers and the Making Strange of Things

The Danish for *King* is *Konge.* You will see the dilemma for a film producer.

I hope to show here something of the complexity, simplicity and wonder of language, and perhaps, as a result, to arrive at an understanding of what language is, especially as a creative art and in its dependence on myth.

First, we have to distinguish between two great, yet separate, linguistic skills: 'translation', which is 'carrying across', and 'interpretation', which is 'trafficking between'.

In my experience, the world's best linguists are Russian. To attend a conference in Moscow, where simultaneous interpretation is provided, is to witness an astonishing performance. The interpreter sits in a booth before a microphone, and, as each speaker delivers, the words pour from the interpreter with no appreciable hesitation. It is done usually with closed eyes, for the sake of concentration, but that makes whatever is taking place appear to be even more mediumistic. Such is the stress, that an

121

interpreter works about a twenty-minute shift. Towards the end, the next interpreter enters the booth and listens, to pick up the rhythm and idiosyncrasies of the speaker. After the twenty minutes, the fresh interpreter slips into the seat and takes over, while the other leaves, and, once out of the booth, collapses with the exhaustion of a ballet dancer coming off stage. Aware of this, I always give the interpreters a copy of what I am going to say a day in advance. It is not because I am kind, but so that they may make their own translations, not interpretations, and I may be the more accurately and the more subtly represented.

I must admit here to being a victim of such admiration.

On my second visit to Moscow, I approached my seat, where my nationality was marked by a card: '*Velikobritannia*', which I think is an improvement on 'Great Britain'. But when I sat down, I saw that on my side of the card was engraved '*Geat Britain*'. How much of *Beowulf* could I improvise? Could I sight-read my paper into Old English? These Russians were quite capable, I was sure, of having Anglo-Saxon scholars in that booth, ready for me. But I trusted in the other side of Russian culture that I had noticed: the innate preference for fiasco. I was right.

In order to approach the nub, I want to say something about the forms of language that are called pidgin and creole. They are often confused, but the difference between them is easily shown.

Two ships collide. The crews reach shore; and find that they have no words in common. A year later, they are rescued, and one thing can be certain: the stranded sailors will be chatting easily among themselves, but the rescuers will understand little that is said. What has happened is that a hybrid has evolved, a pidgin, a contact language. The crews go their separate ways, and, if there is no need for them to meet again, that pidgin will disappear immediately.

If two languages permanently engage (historically it is by conquest or trade), the initial pidgin develops into a language as valid as any other but with a tendency for one culture, in this formative period, to be in some way dominant. The resulting language is a creole; and where the creole still recognisably comprises its differing elements, the result can be mistakenly heard as primitive. The cause is that the dominant element tends to be the vocabulary of traders, seamen, soldiers and the generally foul-mouthed uneducated, while the initially subservient retain their more complex grammar and syntax, forming what is an agglutination; which can be disconcerting.

For instance, in Neo-Melanesian: 'back of the head', 'arse bilong het'; 'helicopter', 'mixmaster bilong Jesus Crist'; 'concertina': 'fella-yu-subim-i-go-fella-yu-pullim-i-go'. This form of agglutination can make sacred texts sound alarming. Yet there is beauty, too. The word for 'vein' is 'rop bilong blut'; 'hair', 'gras bilong het'; and there is the humanity and the humility of 'Forgive us our trespasses' in 'Forgivim wanfella buggarap bilong mifella'. It must be said again: here is a true and complete language, lacking nothing. So let us learn from history. And we must know that the humour works both ways.

A Basque poet told me that Basques are amused by the British apparent concern for vermin. We seem to be eternally keeping them at bay by uttering their name as an apotropaic mantra. The Basque is, in reality, reacting to a habit of the English language of interjecting the word 'sorry' into conversation. 'Sorry' phonetically in Basque means 'body lice'.

But move deeper.

Su. Lur. Zur. Egur. Helur. Elur. Urte. Ur. In the Basque language, for the Basque writer, there is a unity not only of sound but of the expression of the nature of being that is not there for us. *Su*: 'fire'. *Lur*: 'earth'. *Egur*: 'firewood'. *Zur*: 'standing wood'. *Hezur*: 'bone'. *Elur*: 'snow'. *Urte*: 'year'. *Ur*: 'water'. *Ur*, water, the essential for all life, is the modifying principle of life-sustaining words in *earth* that sustains the cycle of the *year*. It is no freak of Basque. It is no coincidence. It is a clear and simple example of connection that every evolved language makes, either plainly, as here, or in its etymologies.

So I can make my first point. Words are metaphor, not statement; metaphor, not simile, which is a quite disparate phenomenon.

Unless words are metaphor, they are dead. You will find this wherever you come across a jargon, which is a valid construct stripped of ambiguity in order to communicate matters precisely, simply and beyond misunderstanding. The words are not elegant and have no literary value. They serve, but never dictate.

It is a different affair when a living language is taken for a superficially similar purpose and mangled to a porridge so that the banal may be profound, the meaningless an insight and the straightforward a complexity, in order to demonstrate the depth of thought and the sensitive insight of its user. The clarity of a true jargon is missing. Instead there is what amounts to intellectual delirium. And for our day, the withered laurels must be given to the world of academe.

It is to the great credit of the USA that an American academic has called a halt. Alan Sokal, a physicist at New York University, was so disgusted by the polysyllabic mish-mash that he wrote a paper that was composed entirely of a string of the most absurd published statements that he could find. He gave the paper the title: 'Transgressing the Boundaries: Towards a Transformative Hermeneutics of Quantum Gravity', and he submitted it to the academic journal *Social Text*, which published it. He was reacting against a translation from nothing into a seeming something.

Although Sokal is a physicist, his true target is the twentieth-century French linguistic philosophers, for whom there is a limited place, since theirs is one, but only one, way of looking.

However, these people have taken it on themselves to become the sole arbiters. Theirs is a tyranny, not a discipline. I encountered them directly in 1997 at the Institut International Charles Perrault, where Professor Jean Perrot, supported by the University of Wales, the University of Massachusetts, Deakin University, Melbourne, and Stockholm University staged a conference entitled: 'The Dreaming of the Aborigines, or Alan Garner's Baroque Apotheosis'. I was instructed to deliver three papers with the preordained titles: 'From the Cave to the Sky: Towards

Dancing with the Rainbow Snake'; 'A Voice that Thunders'; and 'Alan Garner, the New Comus?'

I made my excuses.

When critic and theory have precedence over text, then language is hijacked, and academics that, for whatever reason, embrace such fundamentalism, have, as in all forms of reductive sectarian activity, rejected all that is clear and reasonable. They have rejected proof and logic, which show whether an argument is, or is not, tenable. They have abjured poetry and imagination, and, ultimately, they must deny all but their own view of truth. They are the totalitarians of literacy.

That is why Sokal's paper was published. He had the received blatherskite; which was all that mattered. Judging his argument was irrelevant. By writing the gibberish, the galimatias, the hogwash, the drivel, the translation of nothing into seeming something, Sokal showed that what is said is of no consequence. Indeed, it is better if there is nothing to be said. Given that, one can concentrate on not saying it. I do not exaggerate. University teachers, from all parts of the world, tell me of their concern that the majority of colleagues concentrate primarily on the critic, then on the theory, so that the student is in danger of not seeing the importance of reading the texts that were written, but not written in order to produce theory or to clothe critics.

Robert Graves reported meeting one such naked emperor, who did not feel the cold, since he made more money from what he said that Graves's poetry truly meant than Graves earned from truly writing. With that in mind, I get on with my work, confirmed in the opinion that philately may be the harmless affair of consenting philatelists, but it is not the concern of the postman. Time and again this truth is brought home to me. Story cannot live if it is written to fulfil prejudice. For me, if for no one else, the most important and obscure aspects that I am seeking reveal themselves in flashes of insight that come unbidden.

In the research for *Strandloper* I had tracked down a collateral descendant of my protagonist. He was an old man, reclusive, silent, grim, and died two days after our only meeting.

Yet he had let me into the cottage where he had been born and spent his life because he had played in the same brass band as my uncles and cousins. I helped him to finish his meal, checked that he had taken his medication, brought in coals for the night, and ended up replacing his braces, which had snapped the previous week, by grappling him to me as he held on to the mantelpiece while I slotted a luggage strap three times around his waist. In doing so, I found an essential aspect of my protagonist. The thought went through my head that if the would-be Doctors of Philosophy that write to me asking for opinions on my work and its relationship to structuralism, deconstructualism, phenomenology, semiotics, the objective correlative, the hermeneutic circle, and not least, my debt to Shklovsky's theory of 'ostranneniye' in Russian Formalism: if only they could see that writing lay more in trying to keep an old man's trousers up, and that from such moments came a novel.

Ersatz attempts to communicate ideas fail because they lack poetry and metaphor. I would go further and suggest that we communicate best when we engage with seeming nonsense, because that is poetry and metaphor entire.

'Jabberwocky' is the epitome of British genius. It plays with words and it plays with concepts. It prepares the translator for the linguist's final torture: the pun.

The pun is not mere wordplay. Cultural context is also involved, to make the translator's job harder. Our grandson, days after his sixth birthday, saw a fruit lying squashed where it had fallen. He shook his head, and, in pretended grief, sobbed: 'A damson in distress!' So simple; but what is the translator to do?

Every evolved language is able to say all that it needs to say. It lacks nothing that it can know. The translator has to find a way to carry meaning and metaphor and poetry and substance across and to recreate an equivalent in the other language, with the minimum of loss and the possibility of gain. I have had the privilege of seeing this happen.

A friend, Tatiana Dobronitskaya, a translator from the Scandinavian languages into Russian and *vice versa*, was staying with us on her first visit to England. It was November. The day was gloom. Drizzle fell. Perfect weather for the Slavonic soul. We walked in woodland for several hours, not speaking. Years earlier she had paid me the Russian compliment of saying that I knew the values of silence. It was a scene out of a Bergman film. Then she yelped and ran. She ran to a silver birch and hugged it, and smelt it, and licked it, and stroked it as if it were Braille, and put her forehead, then her cheek, against it, broke off a piece and chewed it. She beckoned and called for me to come to her. She pointed to a blemish on the bark and demanded to be told what it was. I said that it was the effect of a parasitic fungus, very common, which did the tree little harm. 'Now I know the word,' she said. 'Now I know the word.'

It emerged that she had been held up in the translation of a Norwegian novel because she could not understand a metaphorical use of a birch tree. The trouble was that the Russian birch is not affected by this fungus, and so she had not seen the result, until now. Her problem was not botanical. The blemish, in the novel, was being used figuratively to describe a state of mind. She spoke in Russian, not clinically describing the afflicted birch, but forming a new sentence, where she coined a phrase for a loveless marriage, which she called a 'mushroom marriage': one that could be eaten, but without nourishment, or could kill. '*Brak kak berezovik*'. And within the phrase, as she cast it, were phonetic hints at the Russian word for a birch tree, *bereza*. Here is the glory of cross-cultural creativity. Tatiana had brought out the poetry that follows metaphor in all language.

So language is metaphor and poetry, not the packing of a dictionary. Then is it even more? Yes. It is play. This question was answered for me through Nina Demurova, another Russian friend and a global authority on Lewis Carroll, when she coped with the translation of the horrors that await the linguist in the monstrous challenge of *Alice*. One aspect of that challenge will show how superb translation cannot be separated in creative quality from original writing.

The rendering of wordplay is the greatest difficulty. There

is almost no humour in *Alice*. What we have to deal with is verbal wit that, strictly speaking, cannot be overcome. Demurova decided to dare on her own account, to catch the spirit rather than the word.

Carroll: 'Mine is a long and sad tale!' said the mouse, turning to Alice and sighing.
Demurova: 'Mine is a long and sad tale!' said the mouse, turning to Alice and sighing. 'The scoundrel!'

Here is the art of the translator as it should be. Demurova cannot make Russian connect 'tale' with 'tail' directly; so she does something else, different, yet the same. In Russian, *prochvost* is 'scoundrel', and there are the two words, *pro*, 'about' and *chvost*, 'tail'. Which draws from Alice, '"About a tail"? A sad tale about a tail?' Carroll, and Russian, have been well served.

I share some history with Carroll: a birthplace, Cheshire, a background of a common language, and speech impediments; all of which may enable me to experience something that others have not.

At the age of eight, Dodgson attended a trade exhibition sponsored by Francis, Lord Egerton. The exhibition contained many curios and objects of natural history, including a stuffed dodo. It may be asked why, out of so many oddities, a dodo should lay claim to a child's memory. It may be answered that if a child stammers, and his name is Dodgson, a natural affinity would be imprinted immediately.

There is also the near certainty that Dodgson, until he was sent away from family to school, was brought up in those formative phonetic years by servants who spoke in the Cheshire tonality, cadence and vocabulary, while his mother was perpetually concerned with eleven pregnancies and his father, a cleric, with parochial duties.

'Jabberwocky' first emerged in 1855, during a visit to his parental home, under the title 'Stanza of Anglo-Saxon Poetry', but with different definitions and etymologies from those that Dodgson later put into *Alice*. That significance, I allege, points to an amputated man, a man amputated from simple language, and from a land to which he could not return, and from the intimacies of sibling affection. I must stress that I express these thoughts as a writer observing a writer. There is no claim to scholarship. But a writer is tuned to read both the words and the words behind the words.

Here is Dodgson's draft of 1855:

> 'Twas bryllyg, and ye slithy toves
> Did gyre and gymble in ye wabe;
> All mimsy were ye borogoves;
> And ye mome raths outgrabe.

Dodgson then provides a glossary and etymologies of the alleged 'Stanza'. And I shall add my own commentary on the idiolect. All are words known in rural Cheshire, and I myself have used them, or heard them, now, and as a child, without any modification needed.

Dodgson: *Bryllyg.* (Derived from the verb to *bryl* or *broil.*) 'The time of broiling dinner, i.e. the close of the afternoon.'
Cheshire: *Bryl.* 'to boil'.

Dodgson: *Slythy.* (Compounded of *slimy* or *lithe.*) 'Smooth and active.'

Cheshire: *Slither,* 'to slip out of control'; and *lither,* 'lazy'.

Dodgson: *Tove.* 'A species of Badger. They had smooth white hair, long hind legs, and short horns like a stag. Lived mainly on cheese.'

Cheshire: *Toves.* This is a phonetic transcription of *taws,* the plural of *taw,* 'a mischievous child'. In this sense it is always affectionate. My cousin and I would be called in from play by our grandmother with the command: 'Let's be having you, you lithermon taws!' *Lithermon,* 'a lazy fellow', is here used adjectivally, so that the phrase means 'you idle ne'er-do-wells'.

Dodgson: *Gyre.* Verb (derived from *gyaour,* 'a dog'). 'To scratch like a dog.'

Cheshire: *Gyaour!* is the phonetic form of the usual abuse for a dog that gets in the way or is barking without cause. (To *gyre* is 'to suffer from diarrhoea with the intensity of a calf'.)

Dodgson: *Gymble.* 'To screw out holes in anything.'

Cheshire: The verb is 'to make holes with a gimlet'.

Dodgson: *Wabe.* (Derived from the verb to *swab* or *soak.*) 'The side of a hill' (from its being soaked by the rain).

Cheshire: *Swab* is 'to swash liquid'. A *waede* is 'a ford on a stream'.

Dodgson: *Mimsy.* 'Unhappy'.
Cheshire: 'Sombre and affected.'

Dodgson: *Borogove.* 'An extinct kind of Parrot. They had no wings, beaks turned up, and made their nests under sun-dials; lived on veal.'
Cheshire: *Boro.* 'A potato hog'; *gove,* 'the channel in a cowshed or shippon'. (I do not connect that with veal, though others may.) The conflation is no more absurd than the 'extinct Parrott', and Dodgson may have remembered the words without ever having known their meaning.

Dodgson: *Mome.* 'Grave'.
Cheshire: *Mome* and *mommocks.* 'Scraps of food made into a gravy for pigs.'

Dodgson: *Rath.* 'A species of land turtle. Head erect, mouth like a shark, the front fore legs curved out so that the animal walked on its knees; smooth green body; lived on swallows and oysters.'
Cheshire: 'A strong plank running along the top of the side of a farm cart.'

Dodgson: *Outgrabe.* 'Past tense of the verb to *outgribe* (it is connected with the old verb to *grike* or *shrike*).'
Cheshire: To *grike* or to *skrike* is 'to cry as a child'.

Dodgson concludes: 'Hence the literal English of the passage is: "It was evening, and the smooth active badgers were scratching and boring holes in the hill side, all unhappy were the parrots, and the grave turtles squeaked out." This is an obscure, but yet deeply affecting, relic of ancient Poetry.' Is it also an unconscious attempt to hold on to childhood by making of it a disguised creole?

A nearer translation of Carroll's partly corrupt text might be: "Twas boiling, and the idle mischievous lads had diarrhoea as badly as a calf, enough to bore holes in the bed of a ford. All sombre were the potato hogs and the shippon drains, and the pigswill on the edge of the cart cried out.'

I am proposing a model. I know something of Dodgson. I know my native tongue. And I know how writers work. A model, then: a mere suggestion, to explain a boy who spent time in a place where rural words were all about him in the air, but never on a page; words heard in the background, their meaning not explained, yet their sounds not forgotten; a boy of precocious intelligence who became a stammering intellect of great complexity that he could not resolve as Dodgson of Oxford, but instinctively tried to assuage as Carroll of Daresbury, the 'snarky', overly timid 'mardy-arse' who told stories to his sisters (in whose presence he did not stammer), and played the game of 'bandersnur' with his brothers, but who spent his adolescence and adult life among aggressive males, so that he had to become 'boojert', the phonetic value of 'bugert', shape-shifter and trickster, in order to survive.

This is how, as a writer (and Carroll would say that a writer can be wrong), I interpret the stuttering Dodgson of Christ Church, Oxford, who each time he looked out from his rooms could see on the backs of carvings both the stutter and the onomatopoeia of the College masons' traditional mark: 'Ch. Ch.' The Cheshire he once spoke clearly, but never could again, nor could return to in innocence, except through the disguised truth of 'Jabberwocky'. 'A deeply affecting relic of ancient Poetry' it is indeed.

Dodgson-with-Carroll, from Newton-by-Daresbury, are the Cheshire Cat. They will always leave only the grin. For the snark was a boojum, you see.

But what *is* artistic creation?

If psychology were able to show definite causalities in artistic creation, it could be claimed to be a branch of science. The psychologist must always have the right to try to find causality, but find it he will not, because the creative urge is not rational and will refuse all rationalistic approaches. The creative act, being rooted in the immensity of the unconscious, itself named as such by psychology, will dodge all attempts at understanding. It describes itself only in its manifestation; it can be guessed but not grasped.

What I am saying is that the creative mind balances on the edge that divides all art. Art has two extremes of expression, and it is in getting the balance right, for the work, for himself, and for the audience, that the artist's duty lies; and the more daring the high-wire act, carried without mishap, the greater the resulting art. For art is nothing without risk.

From the beginning of human society in the Palaeolithic we find traces of our efforts to banish dark forebodings by expressing them in a magical form, and it continues today. There has never been a culture that did not have a developed system of secret teaching concerning the things that lie beyond earthly existence. The Australian Aboriginal men's and women's councils preserve this knowledge and hand it down in the rites of initiation. The Mysteries of the Graeco-Roman world performed the same function.

It is natural that the artist will turn to myth in order to give accurate expression to experience. Nothing would be more mistaken than to suppose that we are working with second-hand material. The mythic experience is the source of the creativity. In itself it is nothing but a tremendous intuition.

If what I have tried to say has not been said before, I shall be troubled. I hope that am saying nothing new, but I hope more that the way in which I am saying it challenges your view of what words are and that it has been an entertainment. For both story and theory are but entertainment: an invitation to engage, a provocation to respond. And the provocation, the 'calling forth', works both ways. For in trying now to speak the ineffable I have to go within myself to where I mistakenly feel most at risk.

Through nonsense and punning and allusion and play we are shown that words take us beyond metaphor and poetry to a place where words themselves may not speak. They may only reflect. At the end, *in extremis*, we can never say what we mean. The mirror that reflects is metaphor and poetry, but what they reflect is truth; and truth can be expressed by image alone; which is symbol; which is myth. Then myth is truth. That is no sleight of tongue.

By 'myth' I do not mean 'fiction', but more the weaving of patterns that we unconsciously recognise as the core of

being, both within and without us. It is particularly unfor-
tunate that during the earliest stages of English lexicography
the Deist movement in England was influential. They held
that myth was 'the mischievous invention of corrupt
minds'. The opposite is the case. Myth is as near as words,
through poetry and metaphor, can get to the wholeness
of perfect truth.

Yet I owe an explanation to the academics, at whom
you may well think that I was sniping. I am, in their
jargon, a deconstructionalist. I do have an affinity with
Shklovsky's '*ostranneniye*', or 'the making strange of things'.
However, it is a philosophy arrived at by seeming-
serendipity, by an empirical pragmatism, not by a conscious
or slavish following of a school of literature. It is a happy
accident, discovered later, that a writer has to be able to
cope with Russian Formalism equally as with an old man's
trousers. In that integration lies the victory over, and the
achievement of, the self. And from such victory and
achievement a greater good is served: the greater good of
myth.

Then where is myth? Is it independent of us, or is it of
our making? Are we its creators, or its creatures? It appears
to be a philosophical nightmare, but if we radically change
our approach, we may be able to infer a reality.

What a piece of work is a Man? How noble in reason?
That is the question. And I think that the answer may be
'flint'. For a long time the dividing line between *Homo*
and other animals was the definition of *Homo* as the only
tool user. But many animals have been seen to use tools
in order to solve problems. The important difference is
that the tool is used, then abandoned after the problem

is solved; whereas *Homo* makes a tool, and therefore has an image of its intended form before it can exist; and, after use, keeps it. The conclusion we must draw is that *Homo* conceives of a future where others do not.

With the evolution of *Homo sapiens sapiens*, there appear in the archaeological record articles of personal adornment. This is the first hard evidence of an idea of 'self'. When the concept of a future combines with a concept of 'self' it will create knowledge of a personal death.

Also, with the evolution of *Homo sapiens sapiens*, there appears evidence of the ability for complex speech and an accelerated sophistication in the making of tools.

Yet there has always, from the time of *Homo ergaster*, been a remarkable sophistication. Many of the objects appear to be functional only at first sight, but on examination they show that they have been fashioned with delicacy, finesse and control that could have no physical application. They would break. What has happened? I have spent much of my life handling these artefacts, and the conclusion I have reached is that objects were made for a non-practical purpose that we can but guess at, except to say that such objects were fashioned deliberately to have no applied physical use, which raises, for the first time, the question of aesthetics, beauty, art, and the concept of a use in another dimension: a dimension that we are the only animal to have shown evidence of devising, or divining.

Anatomically, at the same time as the expansion of technology, the larynx drops in the throat of mutating *Homo*, a process that is necessary for the production of speech, and is a part of the complex changes in the jaw that came with the movement of the spine in order to produce bipedalism. It is also a potentially fatal mutation, because *Homo sapiens sapiens* has become the only animal that can choke to death on food in the windpipe, since the longer pharynx must double as the route to the alimentary canal. Nor is that all. One of the many results of spinal movement is an overcrowding of the jaw, from which we still suffer: the impacted wisdom tooth. Archaeology shows that, without some form of dentistry, impacted wisdom teeth alone inflict upon the population a mortality rate of between 20 per cent and 25 per cent.

Bipedalism led, in *Homo*, to the possibility for analytical language as opposed to simple vocalised codes, which many animals demonstrate. To have kept that facility suggests that, through language, there must be an essential benefit, perhaps concerned with more than physical survival, with something beyond that other dimension, if the species is to select, in the Darwinian sense, for a change that kills a quarter of its members for certain, and risks even more of those that bolt their food.

But who was the first speaker of what we can call a language? Somebody had to start. I suggest that 'somebody' was not a male adult but a child or children interacting in the casual and highly social activities of female adults in hunter-gatherer societies.

It is recognised that the human brain, during its first ten to fourteen years, is especially adept at acquiring language and languages. Thereafter, the brain has other needs, and new languages become harder to learn. But in childhood the brain experiments and plays and is creative.

139

Remember the damson in distress. Remember the amputated Dodgson whose Carroll remained the child that gave us such linguistic fireworks.

No male adult *Homo* could afford to play with speech. For him the priority was physical survival. His predator had little concern for the Imperfect Subjunctive, and he would have had no use for Conditional Clauses in Indirect Speech in order to catch his prey. Language must have grown as a constructive game of Chinese Whispers, each generation passing on finer and finer tuning. On an evolutionary scale, once the process had begun, it would be but a few steps from a grunt and a clip across the ear to the honing of the Gerund. In the last few moments of hominid prehistory, was it children that opened our ears to the gods?

History, writing, is more a nanosecond on this scale; yet it has already done more than speech could ever do. It carries thought through time and space, linking the mind of the writer with the mind of the reader in a space without time. That is why literature is now a *sine qua non* of human progress. If we do not keep hold of our ability to inform and compare and stimulate and argue and criticise through flexible written words, we shall impoverish our imaginations and our sense of subtlety, and all those flint-toting, choking children will have had more wisdom in their teeth than we in our brains, and the quarter of them that died will have died to no purpose.

Their legacy to us is a timeless vehicle for myth: literature; which they could not have known. The passing on of the finest physical techniques, to the highest levels of abstract thought, is one unbroken line of childhood, from which derives all that is wondrous in words: that effective language is already language translated creatively through play. It is not mundane meaning, but frabjous life, metaphor, ambivalence, organic, myth, poetic, humour, music, true.

18

Dai Shepherd

Dai shepherd dropped his crook, and cried,
  'Enough
Of Llanfairpwllgwyngyllgogeryllogerychwyrn-
  drobwllllantysiliogogogoch!
I'll emigrate to simpler stuff.'
New Zealand beckoned. Off he flew
To tend the sheep of
Taumatawhakatangihangakoauauatamateaturi-
  pukakapikimaungahoronukupokaiwhe-
  nuakitanatahu.

Another man, who lived at Å,
The Norwegian village that rhymes with 'jaw',
Heard of Dai shepherd's gruesome fate.
'That one,' said he, 'leapt soon, looked late.
I'll think about the place for me.'
He went to France; to a farm at Y.

This lecture was given in support of The Magdalen College Bursary Fund on 2 October and to The Oxford University English Faculty on 27 October 2013.

19

The Bull on the Tongue

I am going to try to explain what may be inexplicable: creativity in the modern written word. It entails telling a story; saying something about the act of writing; the nature of language; and why our understanding and use of dialogue has changed during my working lifetime. But it in no way says anything about how to write, because writers have to find that alone; to discover what works for them. The mechanical ability, which we all have, is not enough, any more than the ability to nail two bits of wood together makes a carpenter.

I start at the moment when the inevitable became conscious. This is the story.

I sat on a tree stump and wondered.

I was the product of a fortunate time in history: first-generation tertiary education, by way of a free place at a fine school; then a free place to read Classical Mods and Greats at Magdalen College, to prepare for a life in academia. I worked well enough. I was a successful athlete. I was Antony in a production of *Antony and Cleopatra* at Abingdon Abbey, to broadsheet reviews, with Dudley

Moore as Enobarbus and Kenneth Baker as stage manager – warming up for his later job as Home Secretary. And the director was an infuriating yet inspiring young whipper-snapper. Heady days. Close friends. What could there be to complain of? Yet I felt sick. No one had ever asked me what *I* needed; and I had never questioned. I had complied. Until now. I was on a production line. All I had to do was to be a good boy, enjoy the ride and fulfil the ambitions and expectations of others. Yet much as I loved the ride, it was imperative that I get off, because I knew that what I was doing was wrong.

Although I had intended to be an academic, the work had begun to pall. I was reading some of the best of world literature, but not in the right way; not in the right way for me. I was learning more about less.

The crisis hit when a lecturer was leading us through the textual analysis of the *Agamemnon* of Aeschylus. The play begins with a watchman describing the boredom of waiting for the return of King Agamemnon from the ten-year siege of Troy. Then the signal beacon flares. The waiting is over. Agamemnon is here. The watchman rejoices. But he breaks off, unable to go on; in these words: βοῦς ἐπὶ γλώσσῃ / μέγας βέβηκεν· 'A great bull has come upon my tongue.' I read the words with excitement, but also with terror. At the end of the session, the lecturer asked whether we had questions. I said: Why those words? He answered that my question was outside our terms of reference, and passed on. He was right; but I wanted to yell. Was this the future? Was I a scholar? If not, what?

And here my background, from which society would say I had escaped, saved me. Sitting on the tree stump while waiting for a bus, I looked at a dry stone wall built by my great-great-grandfather, Robert Garner. And I saw.

I come from a line of elitist, perfectionist, manual craftsmen: materially poor, but spiritually independent, refusing to compromise their skills, or to owe obedience to any man. They were makers. I had to follow them; else all I had learnt at school and university was wasted and I should become not a maker but a purveyor. But what could I make?

I could not read music or play an instrument. I could not sculpt, paint or draw. My hands were stupid. But I did have an ability to absorb languages. The answer was clear. I should write.

That reasoning was infantile and fallacious. Yet it tricked me into acceptance, and shielded me from awareness that creativity is not a job. It is a state.

My decision brought the roof in. Well-meaning folk said that I should write – as a hobby; in the evenings; at weekends; during holidays; when I retired. I felt I had left it too late at the age of twenty-one. So I shut up, cut my umbilical cord and looked for somewhere to live. My tutor had said to me, 'You will find that what you have learnt at this place will enable you to do without the money it will have prevented you from earning.' He was not wrong. I found a ramshackle lair, which I recognised as a medieval hall, settled in, and all my work has been written there. But first I had to start.

I looked at the sheet of blank paper. The sheet of blank paper looked at me. It did not intend to help. Indeed, the more I looked, the more it mocked. I had to do something. I wrote a Roman numeral I, in the top right-hand corner.

Nothing happened. There was no thunder on any side. I put an Arabic numeral 1 next to the Roman. No bird, auspicious or inauspicious, cried or flew. And, since this would be either an important or an unimportant moment, I added: 4.03 p.m. Tuesday 4 September 1956. And I began. It was a fantasy. *The Weirdstone of Brisingamen.*

Now if anyone feels compelled to write but is afraid to start, read this, because I challenge you to do as badly at your first attempt.

Colin and Susan Whisterfield, ten-year-old twins, sat in the attic window and gloomily watched the rain slide slowly and stickily out of the dull grey London sky into the dull grey London streets. Every day for nearly a week now the children had been forced to sit indoors and listen to the steady drip, drip, drip of the wet world outside.

'I don't think it's ever going to stop,' said Colin, with his chin on his hands. 'I'm fed up.'

'Never mind,' said Susan. 'There can't be much more rain left in the sky, and a week tomorrow we'll be on our way to Cornwall, so we're bound to have lovely hot sun and blue skies, and we'll look for smugglers and buried treasure and have picnics and bathe in the sea and explore caves and catch shrimps, and—'

'Huh!' said Colin. 'Treasure! Smugglers! There would have been more chance of our finding that sort of thing if we'd lived two hundred years ago. Nowadays there's nothing left to discover.' He little thought that before very long they would meet with things stranger than buried treasure and worse than smugglers; but for the moment he was, understandably, depressed, and it was only slowly that thoughts of the holiday to come kindled his imagination and changed the drab rooftops into rolling Atlantic breakers and the houses across the square into towering Cornish cliffs, like those in the Geography books at school.

The picture was almost complete when Susan suddenly jumped up and said, 'Look, here's Daddy! And it's not even tea time!'

At this point I gagged, struck two lines through the lot and wrote MUSH in capital letters between. Could I, schooled in the highest traditions of Western thought, have perpetrated this? The answer was that I could and I had. I began again. It was worse. I began again. And again. And again. And again.

What was wrong? I backtracked through my thinking; and I saw.

Before going to Oxford I had spent two years in the army as a National Service subaltern, a 'Temporary Gentleman', with nominal command over men twice my age; NCOs that had seen and known more than I ever would; and I had learnt that it was a foolish officer that did not listen to his sergeant.

From there I had entered a world of callow cleverness, of undergraduates younger than I was in every way, who were noisily bent on putting the world to rights, who had all the answers to questions that, from experience rather than abstractions, I was only now beginning to formulate.

How could I, twenty-one years old, write anything of use or interest?

Logic gave me what I thought was the answer. I could not say anything new to the people twice my age; but perhaps those half my age could benefit. Therefore I should write for children. And that had been the juvenile error.

I now realised that, however immature the result, the only way to hope to grow, to say anything both new and universal, was to write for myself and not for some unknowable audience. Yet, at twenty-one, even though I ignored children, I could draw on little other than my own childhood for my material. I did not know how rich and unusual that childhood had been.

The Weirdstone of Brisingamen was two years in the writing, and it was another two years before it was accepted and published; and I was a year into the second book, *The Moon of Gomrath*.

From the middle of *The Weirdstone of Brisingamen* I had felt the work would be a trilogy; simply because there was so much surplus research material. But by 1961, when I was approaching the end of *The Moon of Gomrath*, I could not face spending any more time in the company of Colin and Susan. I had moved on. They had not.

It was during the chapter of the siege of Errwood, a ruined mansion, which regained its original form only when moonlight fell on it, and where the shape-shifting witch-crow, the Morrigan, had imprisoned Colin. I had reached this. (There is no need to know the plot.)

Albanac cantered back to the house, turned Melynlas, and broke into full gallop along the drive. A line of bodachs knelt on the fringe of the dark, but Melynlas swept down on them and, as they couched their spears in the gravel, soared high and safe over their heads into the moonlight which the fires made blind to the children and the elves. All the children knew of what followed was told by the sounds that came to them.

And then Melynlas grew out of the night, foaming and red-hoofed. Uthecar rode behind Albanac, still cutting the air, but Albanac was low over the horse's neck, and a gold-handled sword trailed from his side.

I could not go on. I had had enough. Then something took over, and my hand continued of its own, to produce this temporary, cathartic resolution.

'Yarroo!' cried Albanac. 'I've been got at!' And he dropped dead.

'We wins!' said the Morrigan from the rhododendron bushes. And when the moon came out and the house reappeared, she went up to the room where Colin was and wrung the little bugger's neck. THE END.

I was free. The book, the better for the outburst, recovered and ran to its present conclusion. I was free. Or so I thought.

Thirty-five years later, with the publication of *Strandloper* in 1996, I began to meet mature adults that had read *The Weirdstone of Brisingamen* and *The Moon of Gomrath* as children. And I noticed that those adults often said that they felt that the story was 'not over'; that there was 'unfinished business'; that there was 'a book not written'. I said nothing. I was too embroiled in the writing of *Thursbitch* to think further.

In 2003 *Thursbitch* was out of the way, and I realised that there was unfinished business indeed. The question was: What happened to Colin and Susan after *The Moon of Gomrath*? What happens to children that have experienced another dimension and are then left to grow up in what we call the 'real' world? C. S. Lewis answers this by killing them off. But what if the children are obliged to live? 'What if?' is the preface that both frees and directs the imagination. It is the flange of the wheel, which lets the story run, yet keeps it on the rails. 'What if?' allows anything, but that 'anything' must abide by the rules the 'What if?' generates; otherwise the result is untrue.

My way of working is only one way, perhaps of no practical use to anyone else, ever.

Each book is the first – or ought to be. By this, I mean that any facility gained through experience should be outweighed by one's own self-critical development. The author should become harder to please. Yet there does seem to be a pattern to all.

It is this. An isolated idea or image presents itself spontaneously. It can come from anywhere: something that happens; something seen; something heard. I react to it, usually forget it; but it's filed in the unconscious mind.

Later, and there is no saying when that will be, another idea or image appears, unconnected to the first; and a spark flies between the two. They stand out clearly, together, and I know they will form a book. The moment is involuntary and instantaneous: a moment of particularly sharp vision; but of no understanding.

It is self-delusion, but there is the sense that the book already exists, has always existed, and the task is not invention but archaeological excavation. I must make the invisible object into something that others can see and interpret. That calls for research; to give the object shape and me a compass. This period varies. It has never been less than two years, and the most, to date, ten years. The spark struck by the primary ideas is all that originality is or can be; and the point where hitherto pre-existing yet unconnected themes converge and meet, like the crossing of the poles of a tepee, is where the book waits.

When the research notes start to refer to each other I know that there is no more to be done but to let the story gestate. I become torpid and unintelligent. It is what I call the Oh-my-God bit. I sleep for long periods. I stare into the fire, watching the pattern of flames; waiting. I am not safe to take a sheep down a lane. Yet I have come to recognise that this is the time when the book is being written – by the unconscious. It has switched my brains off so that they do not get in the way. Then, with the jolt of slipping from a kerbstone, I see things happening and hear people talking in the theatre of the head, and I write it down.

I always have little idea of what a story is about, and it feels that I make it up as I go along, though I do not; but there is no conscious plot or structure. I am a spectator.

I watch. The sensation is not so much of an epiphany but that the convecting images, the research, the connections, the dreaming, the years of staring into the fire meld to form a compost to grow the story. It feels that I am not in control, though I am; through the unconscious. It is an organic richness of emotion, uncontaminated by any message, social concern, sermon, dogma or agenda. If it is anywhere near right, each reading should produce a different creative response in the reader, who will see things I did not.

Over more than half a century, I have developed the argument that creativity takes place in the unconscious; which is to beg the question of its existence; but it works for me, and that is what counts. The conscious intellect, which I was educated to venerate, and do not despise, is a fine analyst, but now is not its time.

When the words are flowing, I am the conductor, not the source: a piece of copper wire, not the generator.

'Spark.' 'Kerbstone.' 'Gestation.' 'Tepee.' 'Theatre.' 'Spectator.' 'Archaeology.' 'Compost.' 'Copper wire.' How many metaphors have I used in trying to explain what I do not understand? It is absurd. But is it?

If creativity is the product of the unconscious, as it appears to be with me, then, since I am the instrument of the work, I am subordinate to it, and cannot interpret it. I cannot say what it 'means', even if I want to. I have done my best by giving it form, translating it, and must leave interpretation to others and to the future.

I am reluctant to look at anything once it is in print. When I hold the finished book I open it to see that the international copyright sign is in place, next to my name, which proves that the book exists and that I wrote it; and then I close it. I know that if I were to read the text I should find a compositor's error and/or one of mine. But twice I have had to look: when adapting *The Owl Service* and *Red Shift* for television.

I arrived on location one morning near the end of the nine-week shoot of *The Owl Service*. Something was different, wrong. The crew were sunbathing. The director asked me whether I had seen the schedule. I had. We were going to film Roger enlarging his photographs in the darkroom he had rigged up.

The director agreed. He then pointed out that several weeks ago we had gone to some lengths to establish that the house had no electricity. How then, he asked, was Roger going to use his enlarger?

But everyone was relaxed. What had happened?

The chief electrician had seen my mistake; and had already covered for it.

Thinking as a film technician, not as a writer, he said that we had established that the adult character, Clive, a city dweller, was not happy in such a godforsaken place. It would be in his character to have a spare battery for his car. The car was featured in the opening sequences, and he, the technician, knew that the battery needed for that car was capable of powering a photographic enlarger. All that was wanted from me was a quick rewrite of directions so that the scene in the darkroom had the battery linked to the equipment and artistically placed in the forefront of the framing; then no clever viewer could whinge. And no reader has felt the need to point out the gaffe; yet.

That is why I do not browse the finished book.

'What's it like? Writing?' people say. 'Do you enjoy it?' It would be futile to tell them it is the research that I enjoy: the discovery and bringing together of pre-existing elements that have not been seen to connect before. I do not invent. I do not go looking for stories. The stories come looking for me. Or that's how it seems. It puts off the moment when the research has to be paid for, when there is nothing left to do but to sit in front of that blank page and spoil it with my pen. And I do mean pen. Words cannot come to life for me in the monotonous lacklustre click of the keyboard of a computer. Creativity is organic and kinetic; I have to feel the words move and join in the flow of hand and arm; and the elbow is a good editor.

I have said that creativity is a state. I am serious. For me there is no option. Writing is what I am.

From time to time people ask for advice on how to write; what is the secret? I answer, and it is true, that there is no secret. If you are a writer, nothing will stop you; and if you are not a writer, nothing can make you one. A deeper truth is that 'I' does not know how to write.

Samuel Beckett, in *Worstward Ho*, put it neatly: 'Ever tried. Ever failed. No matter. Try again. Fail again. Fail better.'

At least that is short. But notice how Beckett speaks of trying and of failing. What he describes is that coming of the bull on the tongue: the vision of something he cannot express, yet must. That is the juice of creativity. The rest is not our business.

It is our business, though, to ask something of the nature of creativity.

Jung sees two different forces at work in creativity, which he calls the 'observational' and the 'visionary'. My experience is the same, and I am extending the argument here.

The two extremes, Jung writes, work with materials taken from the everyday: with emotions, suffering, passion, human fate. All this is assimilated by the creative mind, raised from the commonplace to the level of poetic experience and expressed with a power of conviction that gives a greater depth of insight. The raw material of the 'observational' kind of creation comes from our being alive, from our eternally repeated joys and sorrows, but clarified and transfigured.

Many literary products belong to this class of the 'observational': didactic poetry and all the novels dealing with love, the family, crime and society. Charles Dickens is an instance. The contents derive from conscious human experience. Everything they embrace belongs to the realm of understandable thought. What you see is what you get.

In 'visionary' creativity, all is reversed. The 'visionary' is something strange that derives from the hinterland of being and surpasses our understanding. This is what gives it its value and its impact. Sublime, filled with meaning, chilling, arising from timeless depths, daemonic, grotesque, psychotic, it challenges our human standards of value. Yet this can be a revelation, or a vision of beauty that we can never put into words. It makes quite other demands on the power of the writer than does the foreground of life. It rends the curtain upon which is painted the picture of an ordered world, and allows a glimpse of things not seen. William Golding is an exemplar.

In dealing with the 'observational' creation, we need never ask what the material consists of or what it means. But this question forces itself upon us when we turn to the 'visionary'. We are astonished, confused, bewildered, or even repelled. Yet the writer, working in this way, can never forget the obligation to translate. The readers demand connection. They are reminded of little in their daily lives, but rather of dreams, and the uncanny recesses of the mind.

Since the expression can never match the vision, the writer, in order to communicate at least something, must have a huge store of material to draw on in order to tell, through imagery not description, a fraction of what is glimpsed. That is why the visionary-biased mind can't be as prolific as the observational. So much must be hoiked from within. Here intelligence will not go.

Above everything, however, whether observational or visionary, creativity is risk. Without risk, there can be no progress.

It may be helpful to say something of what I have learnt and observed, so far, as a delver in the word-hoard.

First. A living language is always evolving. If it were not, then in English 'silly' would still mean 'blest'. But an exponent of language is also its guardian. I am no linguistic Luddite. Yet, to take an example, American English has lost the distinction between 'for ever', two words, and 'forever', one word. British English has not, and remains the richer. The rule is simple. If change expands and refines, it is good. If it narrows or reduces, it is not.

Next. English is a bewildering tongue. English, at the moment, has a vocabulary of about a million words, exceeding any other. The reasons for this are historical. What began as a Germanic dialect touched on Celtic, and absorbed the Romance, through Latin, reinforced by its daughter, French. Britain's role as a trading nation, followed by colonial expansion, attracted global influence. 'Pyjama' and 'bungalow' are Hindi; 'canoe' is Carib; 'tea' is a Malayan borrowing from Chinese. 'Cooee' is Kulin Aboriginal Australian: 'come'. And so on.

One result of such a huge vocabulary is that English prose is sensitive to repetition to a degree that many languages are not. For instance, unless it is a part of the structure, I will not use the same colourful or powerful word twice in a novel. It would jar. I must find an alternative to fit the rhythm and surrounding cadences.

This leads to another observation.

English turns to its Germanic roots when we want to be direct, close, honest. The Romance roots are used when we want to keep feeling at a distance, so that we may polysyllabically articulate with precision. Compare 'love' with 'amity'; 'hate' with 'animosity'; 'near' with 'proximate'; 'thanks' with 'gratitude'; 'fear' with 'trepidation'. And Romance words, piled up, form a screen to hide what is said. Coupled with linguistic folly, they are the bane of every committee. Extreme cases are to be found in American military gobbledygook. Here, when a plane crashes, it is reported as being 'functionally disabled'; death is 'zero survivability situation'; bomb is 'energetic disassembly device'; mass murder is 'population and spatial control through kinetic force'; 'kill' is 'terminate with extreme prejudice'; and we do not see human flesh in 'maximise harassment and interdiction'.

The importance cannot be overstated. Language must be clear and simple if it is to communicate, especially if what it is communicating is complex or new.

That is why I tend to prefer words from Germanic roots

when writing narrative prose. Every word has to count; there is no room for passengers. Adjectives are superfluous, and adverbs show that I have not thought enough about what I am trying to say. Which means that when adjectives and adverbs are used, the effect is strong. That is my style, which has developed through experience. Its origins are an education in Latin and Greek, on the bedrock of Old and Middle English, which survives in the native dialect of my childhood, despite a teacher's making me wash out my mouth with soapy water at the age of six because I was 'talking broad'.

We each have our arsenal of language to draw on, and by being true to it we each have our own voice, with no need to ape that of others.

The writer must work with that personal voice: as the craftsman in control and aware of the material, while respecting it, just as the carpenter needs to command the scarf joint, mortise and tenon, the sliding hidden dovetail in the grain that give him the satisfaction of the thing well made and the observer the pleasure of experiencing the art of the wood. In the same way, the writer must be both medium and master of language. Only when grammar, syntax, spelling, punctuation are learnt and understood can their rules be bent, even broken. Literature is born from the controlled tension between the formal and the inventive, which is language at play; but creatively so.

In prose, this is especially true for dialogue at the moment: 'the moment' being about the last sixty years.

When the portable tape recorder became commonly available in the early 1950s it was possible to hear, catch, replay and edit the words and rhythms of everyday natural speech with ease. For writers of talent a new world opened: for example, Samuel Beckett's *Krapp's Last Tape*; and the British stage was revolutionised by John Osborne's *Look Back in Anger* and the work of Harold Pinter.

The Royal Court Theatre in London became the natural home for this new writing. Here Anthony Page cut his teeth and went on to work with Beckett, Osborne and Pinter; Anthony Page, who as that infuriating yet inspiring whippersnapper directed the Magdalen Players' production of *Antony and Cleopatra* in 1956.

The tape recorder released regional and socially diverse voices from music-hall travesty into British mainstream culture. No longer did shop assistants speak on stage and film with the cut-glass modalities of RADA.

All this enabled the popular voice to be heard at a time when television was getting into its stride. It is hard to understand now how much the nation was in shock, and in some quarters incensed, at the arrival of *Coronation Street*.

Lowborn young men and women that had benefited from the Golden Age of the 1944 Education Act were released into the Arts. I was of their generation.

In my first two books I could not handle dialogue. The formal was wooden and the vernacular a mess of phonetic spelling, bespattered with apostrophes. But by the third novel, *Elidor*, I had begun to find my voices.

After *The Weirdstone of Brisingamen* was published, through media attention I discovered that I also had the ability to express myself by using a film camera. I also began to learn to listen, and to use what I heard. And in *Elidor* it shows.

When *Red Shift* was published in 1973, the critics did not know how to react. The initial consensus was that it was not a novel but a script. It was not, but I saw that I had moved from strength in narrative to a preference for dialogue. So when, having had the experience of transferring *The Owl Service* from book to film, I had to do the same for *Red Shift*, I thought it would be relatively easy. The spoken words were already there.

I could not have been more wrong.

The *Owl Service* script saw few changes, and was written in months. *Red Shift* went through more than a year of many drafts. The dialogue had not only to be replaced but restructured. I found that the word on the page is not the same word in the air.

The word on the page, in dialogue, is doing many things. To take that word straight from the page and put it before the camera is to risk overstatement and the absurd, when the camera is already showing what the word says. And dialogue itself, however apparently natural, is at all times an artefact, not a recording. Listen to what is going on around you when you are next at a party. It will be fragmented verbal and intellectual chaos; mediated by laughter and body language. If the writer does not understand that difference, the result is trash.

This shows especially in the use of sexual obscenity.

In common speech the sexual obscenity is an indicator of a barren vocabulary, an intensifier of emotion, or an affectation. It flies and is gone. In the theatre and on film it has more residual and invasive force, through being directed at an unknown, heterogeneous audience; hence the television caveat: 'Contains strong language.' On the page, however, its effect is more. What, when spoken, is transitory is now concrete; and it can be read again.

That is why, I would argue, sexual obscenity in fiction risks being an assault: an act of insensitivity. That is not to ban the words; but the writer should understand their printed force. I am not saying, 'Don't do it.' I am saying, 'Know what you're doing.'

Yet the word caught in the air has enriched more than it has hurt. The grammar and syntax of film and television (particularly in soaps and advertising) have changed the pace and rhythm and texture of written prose.

The aesthetic of modern film directors has also increased the rapidity of editing. Between 1930 and 1960 the average shot ranged from seven to ten seconds. In the early 2000s the length is three to six. Also, there has been marked recourse to zoom lenses, and close position of the camera during dialogue, moving from a cinema of bodies to one of faces. This has influenced the word on the page, so that, in a disciplined hand, the result can be a choreography made new. More can be said with less.

The effect of the tape recorder on dialogue, and of the modern visual impact on narrative, may be shown by comparing an example from either side of the watershed.

In the nineteenth century there was no immediate device for capturing and understanding natural speech. And here, without criticism, is an example of how, before the tape recorder and the 1944 Education Act, stories were told in print; and then an example of the change that was brought about.

Scholars have compared my work and concerns to those

of Thomas Hardy; and we do have much in common: a background of a family of craftsmen in a special place with a native speech that we respect. A significant difference may be that Hardy was an autodidact, and I am not.

Sixty years before the tape recorder, in *Tess of the d'Urbervilles*, Hardy wrote this. Notice the prolixity of both dialogue and narrative.

'Tell me, tell me!' he said, passionately clasping her, in forgetfulness of his curdy hands: 'do tell me that you won't belong to anybody but me!'

'I will, I will tell you!' she exclaimed. 'And I will give you a complete answer, if you will let me go now. I will tell you my experiences – all about myself – all!'

'Your experiences, dear; yes, certainly; any number.' He expressed assent in loving satire, looking into her face. 'My Tess has, no doubt, almost as many experiences as that wild convolvulus out there in the garden hedge, that opened itself this morning for the first time. Tell me anything, but don't use that wretched expression any more about not being worthy of me.'

Twenty years this side of the tape recorder, I could write a different kind of dialogue, helped by the experience of film.

The book is *Red Shift*. Tom and Jan are teenage lovers. Note how the narrative is able to switch points of view within a paragraph, first as omniscient narrator, describing Jan, then as subjective Tom: the closeness of the camera in dialogue, and the crash zoom lens.

They stood in the shelter of the tower, holding each other, rocking with gentleness.

'I love you,' said Jan.

'I'm coming to terms with it.'

'– love you.'

'But there's a gap.'

'Where?'

'I know things, and feel things, but the wrong way round. That's me: all the right answers at none of the right times. I see and can't understand. I need to adjust my spectrum, pull myself away from the blue end. I could do with a red shift. Galaxies and Rectors have them. Why not me?'

Jan wanted no more than to hold him. His words vented. Meaning meant nothing. She wanted him to let the hurt go. He could talk for ever, but not stop holding her. Each second made him less dangerous. And she's not even listening. Why can't I use simple words? They don't stay simple long enough to be spoken. I have not come to terms with her eyes or the smell of her hair.

What happened to Colin and Susan after the end of *The Moon of Gomrath*? The question provoked by adults in 1996 took eight years to answer: from 2003 to 2011. It was *Boneland*. And in doing so a trilogy spanning fifty-five years was completed. People asked: Why did it take so long? The only answer I could give was: Because that is how long it took. But the true answer is: I had to write six other books first. It is not just a trilogy. The nine novels are all one unconscious arc, forming a single work that is resolved and consummated in the last line of *Boneland*; which I did not see until it ran off my pen and was done.

Was that it? Was that the lot? Had I finished? Who could tell? And yet.

I was walking with a friend across the Iron Age fort of Castle Hill, above Huddersfield. He said something inconsequential about a tramp who used to work around the farms near Slaithwaite. This tramp claimed to be able to heal all ills except jealousy. His name was Arthur Helliwell, but he was known as 'Treacle Walker'. I looked at my watch. At seven minutes past three, on the afternoon of Sunday, 15 July 2012, unexpected, unbidden, out of nowhere, a great bull had come upon my tongue.

20

House by Jodrell

Across the field astronomers
Name stars. Trains pass
The house, cows and summer.
Not much shows but that.
Winter, the village is distant,
The house older
Than houses and night than winter.
The line is not to London.
Unfound bones sing louder,
Stars lose names,
Cows fast in shippons wise
Not to be out. I know
More by winter than by all the year,
And in the marrow of the bones I write.

21

Powsels and Thrums

I read somewhere of a shepherd who, when asked why he made, from within fairy rings, ritual observances to the moon to protect his flocks, replied: 'I'd be a damn' fool if I didn't!'

I wish I had written that, but it was Dylan Thomas in his introduction to *Collected Poems 1934–53*.

Here I want to say something about creativity in the Arts: its nature, its power; drawing on what I have learnt over a life spent engaged with words: the nature and power of story. And it is through story rather than argument that I am speaking now.

But first, a requirement of creativity must be made clear. Creativity, whether in the humanities or in the sciences, is play. The creative mind keeps hold of childhood.

The experience of spending a life engaged with words has shown me that nothing is new; and what we call 'creativity' is the bringing together of pre-existing entities in ways that have not been seen to connect before. Here is an example.

While rummaging through a dustbin in 1956 I came upon a newspaper report. Two lovers quarrelled in a pub. He threw a tape at her and left. A week later he killed himself. Only then did she think to play the tape. It was an apology; but he said that if she did not care enough to listen within the week he would know that he had ruined everything. I kept the report. And forgot it.

Nine years later, in 1965, a friend told me a story she had heard from her grandmother. She said that 'long ago' a group of 'Spanish slaves' who were being marched north 'to build a wall' had escaped and settled on Mow Cop, on the Cheshire/Staffordshire border. The unrecorded disappearance of *Legio Nona Hispana*, the Ninth 'Spanish' Legion, at about the time of the building of Hadrian's Wall, is an enigma in the Roman occupation of Britain.

Below Mow Cop lies Barthomley. On Christmas Eve 1643, the church was the scene of one of the grimmest acts in the grimmest conflict on English soil: the seventeenth-century Civil Wars. A troop of Royalists attacked the village. The parishioners fled to the church.

The Royalist commander reported: '[W]ee presently beat them forth of it, and put them all to the sword, which I find to be the best way to proceed with their kind of people, for mercy to them is cruelty.'

In 1966 I was reading graffiti on Alderley Edge station. One, done in chalk, was: 'Janet Heathcoat = Alan Flask. It is true.' Somebody had added, in silver lipstick, without punctuation or a capital letter: 'not really now not any more'. And the sky fell in. The result was the novel *Red Shift*, finished in 1972.

'not really now not any more'. Why should those words at once bring into my mind the forgotten newspaper report, the Ninth 'Spanish' Legion and the massacre of Barthomley? It is how the novels arrive. I do not go looking for them. They come looking for me. That is the feeling. It is mysterious; yet I do not think it is mystical.

Our conscious thought structures are based on rationality, on logic, analysis, on cause and effect. Without them, all would be a shambles, and we should not be intelligent; or not intelligent in that way. Intelligence, however, takes more than one form. There is the linear, which enables us to deal with the material world as we perceive it; and there is the intuitive, over which we have no conscious control. It is this latter intelligence that is the source of creativity.

The intellect is not creative. Here, it is a drudge. Creativity is not polite. It barges in unsought, uninvited, unannounced, confusing, chaotic, demanding, overwhelming, drowning reason and common sense – and leaves the intellect to clean up the mess.

The onrush of creativity as it wells from the unconscious can be frightening. The apparently spontaneous moment sometimes arrives not in the form of an idea but of an answer. The task then is to discover the question. The artist has to trowel backwards, as in an archaeological dig.

More than intuition and play, or trowelling backwards, creativity is risk: heedful risk; but risk entire. Without risk we have the ability only to repeat ourselves, to deny the future. But how does creativity work?

I shall try to explain; and begin by using moments that

formed me beyond their moment, which became linked in the unconscious, just as the newspaper, the graffito, Mow Cop and Barthomley were warp and weft on a loom: a loom of story. They are fragments to show how creativity makes connections between entities in ways that have not been seen to connect before – what my great-great-great-grandfather, Joseph Garner, weaver, would have called 'powsels and thrums'.

Powsels and thrums are the oddments of thread that were kept for personal use, their hues forming new patterns; the oldest of scraps, made into other garb; the oldest of stories, made into other tales.

Story invites the audience to engage; to reach its own creative interpretations. And that is what I am offering now: powsels and thrums.

Dylan Thomas continues: 'These poems, with all their crudities, doubts and confusion, are written for the love of Man and in praise of God, and I'd be a damn' fool if they weren't.'

I was lying on my army bed when Graeme came in, his boots clumping on the floorboards, and said, 'Dylan Thomas is dead.'

In the reign of Tiberius, Thamus, an Egyptian sailor, heard a voice call to him across the water: 'Thamus, are you there? When you reach Palodes, tell them the great god Pan is dead.'

I looked at the barrack-room ceiling. The great god Pan was dead.

Dylan Thomas drank himself to death at the age of thirty-nine. A woman that had known Thomas at primary school told me that he was unpopular, obscene, mean-spirited, sly, a liar and a cheat. His daughter Aeronwy, in our only but long conversation, described the family atmosphere as 'demonic'.

Dylan Thomas's wheedling is well documented, and when I was an undergraduate at Magdalen College, Oxford, the tales of him there were still fresh. He had beguiled the wife of the historian A. J. P. Taylor to persuade her husband to allow Thomas the use of their College house so that he might express his genius in tranquillity. And he was a figure to be avoided as he sought to cadge booze money from undergraduates, dons and staff alike.

In Thomas you have the cartoon of creativity: someone that sweats through the night with an overflowing ashtray and a dwindling bottle. But Aeronwy insisted that her father wrote sober. It was when he had finished that the brakes came off.

Where, then, was the love of Man and the praise of God?

The importance of Dylan Thomas here is that he shows in the extreme the difference between the work and the artist: a tension that may be found wherever creativity takes hold of a life. Creativity does not determine the nature of the artist, who can be as petty, duplicitous and destructive as anyone, however generous, honest and enriching the work. Which is why meeting an artist known only through the work can be disconcerting, when we are more likely to be confronted by, at best, an unremarkable lump of humanity. Yet expectations are hard to shift.

Once, at a conference, a Jungian psychologist refused

to speak to me. He avoided eye contact. When my wife challenged him, he said, 'It's not safe to meet those that have looked into the white-hot crucible of creativity.' I rather like that; and I have been trying to get domestic mileage out of the crucible ever since, but my family appears to be fireproof.

Artists can be as flawed in their personal lives as any other human. Yet in their work they are driven, and ruthless – with themselves and with others.

I watched a builder laying bricks. When he had finished, he stood back, looked at what he had done, tore down the lot and began again. I asked him what was wrong. He said that the bottom course, which was underground, was a quarter of a brick out. I said it had no effect on the structure and would never be seen. He said: 'But *I'd* know.' That, for me, epitomised the artist. Creativity is not a job. It is a state of being. It is service to something beyond the self. In this broad sense, it partakes of the religious.

Powsels and thrums.

As an infant, I was adopted by three teenage girls, who lured me to Sunday school at what we knew as the Tin Mission because it was made of corrugated iron. It was the province of intense young men and women, under the guidance of Mr Bird, a lay preacher of Gaunt Prophet appearance, who had spent much of his career in the Middle East and could make the landscape of the Bible come alive. Later, he gave me a grammar of Ancient Egyptian, which enabled me to keep a diary in hieroglyphics, so that my mother could not read it.

Of the three girls my favourite was Eileen Harwood.

I always held her hand on the way to Sunday school. The trudge towards the Tin Mission was measured by the tightening of Eileen's hold and the increasing volume of the tolling bell. One afternoon, the tocsin became unbearable, and I broke loose and ran home, shouting, 'I'm fed up with that Jesus Christ!'

And so it was; until I reached the age when I could be confirmed into the Church of England. I had no interest in, or desire for, the initiation. But Alderley Edge church needed to maintain its rota of servers at Holy Communion; and it was decreed that I be prepared for the Anglican puberty rite of Confirmation.

The vicar was Mr Leaman: kind, warm, gentle, a good priest, not seeking trouble. But I gave him trouble by formally debating his every doctrinal instruction. Mr Leaman was no more prepared for this than I was for Confirmation, but he kept his nerve. And that is how I came to drink sour wine on an empty stomach on Sundays at eight o'clock in the morning.

There was one noteworthy incident.

In the nineteenth century the merchants of Manchester built their villas on Alderley Edge. The Anglicans erected a church, with steeple; and the Methodists their chapel, with a steeple taller than the church's, housing a clock, which my grandfather wound and fettled for fifty-seven years. The Anglicans 'adjusted' their steeple to be taller than the chapel. The result was a Neo-Gothic needle that could not hold bells.

By the time I was lurching to Communion a loudspeaker system had been installed, linked to a gramophone in the vestry, playing recordings of peals at seventy-eight scratchy revolutions a minute. Harry Smith, the verger, was in charge; but his hearing was not of the best.

On the noteworthy day I set out to prepare the altar. Communicants were making their way to church. In the vestry, Harry switched on the gramophone. And Danny Kaye crooned out across the parish.

> 'Madam, I like your crêpe suzette.
> I think your crêpe suzette is wonderful.
> But for the moment let's forget
> All about your crêpe suzette.'

I staggered.

> 'Madam, I like your cheese soufflé.
> I think your cheese soufflé is wonderful.
> But when you look at me that way
> How can I eat cheese soufflé?'

I was hyperventilating. Danny continued. When the record ended, Harry began again.

I noted four things. The people on the road gibbered. I honked. The vicar conducted the ceremony unflustered. And something happened. The congregation became still. My hands, which had struggled to hold the taper to the candles, were quiet when I presented the water and the wine. Something had happened. The Book of Common Prayer. The 'comfortable' words, by their being spoken, brought calm. It was the moment when I both felt and understood the invincibility of words. Through Danny Kaye I found language.

National Service and Oxford followed. I loved, and love, Oxford. But I came to realise that I was on the wrong path and had to get off it. I had to leave. In a brutal epiphany I saw that, instead of using language to probe Greek and Latin texts, the work lay elsewhere: with my native people, *our* language, *our* land. I had to write. So I did; ignoring the panic of elders, and quelling mine.

Powsels. And thrums. Another story.

A businessman from an ancient culture told me that he could not abide California. The reason was that, for him, modern California has no identity. He said: 'Even the light is a Hockney painting.' That is the power of art. California now reflected David Hockney; not the other way round. The creative mind, in whatever medium, makes the subject personal through the intensity of the vision. Art makes people feel.

At the Giant Redwood Park of Muir Woods, near San Francisco, I met the shallow dimension. In 1930 a redwood fell. A section was cut from it and the rings were marked with historical events. The tree dated from 906, a hundred and sixty years before the battle of Hastings.

I watched as modern Americans went by. They were of several ethnic origins, each having lost their culture. All that concerned them were the rings beneath the immediate sapwood, with no references to anything outside the United States. They had earlier histories, but those histories had been chopped. The Americans were rootless. A party of Japanese arrived; and they pointed to all the dates, back to the tree's heart. And I had to get home. 'Home', here, does not mean a house. In Russian the word is *rodina*.

Rodina is the land, our life force. If we were to be taken from it we should know only the dead slab of the fallen wood.

David Hockney is not alone. Through the intensity of the creative vision, artists magnify the land. William Wordsworth 'discovered' the Lake District. Thomas Hardy recorded his *rodina* as 'Wessex'. J. R. R. Tolkien differed, in that he drew on his youth for *The Lord of the Rings*, but did not identify his sources, with their origins in the West Midlands and, through trauma, extending into his psyche as a landscape of fantasy. The intensity remained; yet, because it was not tied to an attainable place, it was expropriated by New Zealand's travel industry. Now, tourists cross the globe and queue to walk where cinematic Frodo trod, urged by the tagline *Discover your inner Hobbit*.

Association can be grotesque. The *Times Literary Supplement* of 21 February 2014 (p. 29, col. 1) advertised a 'Writer's Retreat': a dwelling in a village where Virginia Woolf allegedly began her first novel. She did not live there. No claim is made for the dwelling other than that it is in the village. Rental included Wi-Fi and a supply of paper. This was not intensified vision. This was sympathetic magic: peddling creativity by contagion.

Art has another force: it communicates the incomprehensible.

We seek to pin down the Universe. The current estimate of its age is about thirteen point seven five thousand million years. But are we any more aware of the immensities as a result of the numbers?

'We' are the questing ape. The quest is what brought

us out of Africa. But our brain has overtaken our body, and mind goes where flesh cannot. We have to interpret what we cannot touch. For that we need intelligence and imagery. Intelligence observes the immensities; imagery translates them.

> Far, far from here, over seven mucky middens, beyond thrice nine lands, beyond the Tenth Kingdom, on the island of Buyan, there is a crystal mountain, sixteen miles high, sixteen miles wide and sixteen miles long. Every thousand years, a little bird comes and wipes its beak, once, on the crystal mountain and flies away. And when the little bird has worn the crystal mountain to the sea, then will have passed the first second of Eternity.

Imagery gives emotional understanding. The little bird, the crystal mountain; they stay with us when the zeros blur. Imagery, art, inform science. They are the two weaves of creativity. And, for the fabric to hold, we need them both. We need them both, if we are to hold the beauty.

Since 1957 I have lived and worked in a medieval house on a burial mound four thousand years old. And the site has been occupied since the end of the latest Ice Age, ten thousand years ago. When I came to live on the mound, I coincided with the completion, three fields away, of the Lovell telescope. We began together.

Powsels and thrums.

Having lived next to the telescope since 1957, I knew its every move. But to understand the art, not the science, I had to know its sounds and textures. I had to get closer.

I wrote to Sir Bernard Lovell. An appointment was made. How was I to convince him of my need?

I arrived, and was shown to his office. Sir Bernard was at his desk, and invited me to sit down. He was affable, but there was no mistaking his eyes.

Sir Bernard asked how he could help, and I said that I wanted to show him something. I took an Early Bronze Age polished stone axe, three and a half thousand years old, out of my briefcase, put it on his desk and said, 'This is the telescope.' Sir Bernard looked at the axe, ran his hands over its surfaces – and gave me a pass to Jodrell.

Later, I heard an account of the meeting from his point of view. 'He came in,' said Sir Bernard, 'and put this "thing" on my desk. I thought it was a bomb.' Which, in a way, it was. Although I did not know it at the time, it was the start for me of 'Operation Melting Snow', of which Jodrell must now be considered *the* exemplar.

'Operation Melting Snow' is the coining of physicist Professor Robert Cywinski to mend a false cleft in our culture. C. P. Snow, scientist and novelist, warned in 1956 that science and the humanities no longer spoke to each other. The result was that Snow was branded as father of the Two Culture Society, which became a received truth in public perception. But, by founding these lectures, Jodrell has given 'Operation Melting Snow' a base from which to repudiate and to refute the schism.

I had not seen that Sir Bernard Lovell was ahead of me when I put the bomb on his desk. I should have known. Sir Bernard was a cosmologist and risk-taker – and church-goer. He was the parish organist. He played at my father's funeral. When he found that his vision and creation, the telescope, was being subverted to political and military ends he considered entering the priesthood – but a bishop said he would do more good by staying where he was, since creativity is prayer.

'Creativity is prayer.' Is that what Dylan Thomas was saying, too? 'These poems are written for the love of Man and in praise of God.'

Philosophy persuades me that belief and unbelief are not open to proof; while anthropology shows that no human society is known to have existed without a sense of the numinous, in the form of ancestors, spirits, gods, God. Why?

Psychologically, prayer may be seen as dialogue with the numinous, and we may need to give the numinous form in order to speak to it, whether as a bearded old man, a rock, a pool, a cave, a bone, or, as one rector of Barthomley told me he saw Christ, a vertical blue laser.

In a mechanistic Darwinian world, can the numinous have an evolutionary application?

In 1975, geographer Professor Jay Appleton published his 'Prospect-Refuge' theory. I am taking it further.

Consider this. Is there anybody that has not felt, at some time, immediately and without reason, that a particular spot, be it landscape or structure, is a 'good' place, and conversely that another is 'bad'? For instance, it would be hard for me to enter Glen Coe. There is a house near Cambridge that I had to force myself to stay in while visiting it. There is a church in which I would not spend time alone. And I defy you to be at ease in a multi-storey carpark. Where I live, where I knew on sight

I had to live, fulfils the criteria for a 'good' place; and gives one explanation of why it has been occupied for ten thousand years.

Appleton's theory has a simple premise: that aesthetics is based on senses that evolved for the survival of bipedal savannah apes; that is, us. We need to see and to be not-seen. We need to feel safe. Places with a clear view give prospect, while places to hide offer refuge. Unless they are in harmony, we do not feel safe.

In the Pleistocene epoch, beginning some three million years ago, the forerunner of *Homo sapiens sapiens* was faced with savannah: grassland that contained prey and predator, dotted with trees and provided with water. In order to benefit from this environment and to survive, *Homo* had to stand up. This freed the hands for carrying tools.

Other animals have tools. Chimpanzees use stones for cracking nuts; birds use them for breaking shells. But they, having got their food, drop the stone, and the next time they feed they have to find another. *Homo*, with hands free, can keep the stone, use it again – and can adapt it. That is the difference that has resulted in the chimpanzee still with the stone and us with the telescope. Yet the savannah has remained a part of our being.

In the Age of Reason, we set the savannah on a pedestal, or rather, a pedestal on the savannah. Landscape was Capability Browned into parkland, where, from prospect of the terrace, with refuge of the mansion, Enlightenment Man took pleasure in his command of Nature. But nothing had changed. Nor has it.

The gardens of suburbia are each a savannah, kept by a clever ape, who mows the grass against predation, dots the middle distance with vegetation for refuge and installs pools, adorned with synthetic gnomes and ducks, surrogates of gods and prey. Garden centres are cradles for a manicured Pleistocene.

Here at Jodrell we can complete a circle, bigger than the dish, and step onto true savannah; the savannah of the arboretum.

Could the prospect-refuge theory influence our reading of reality in those immensities?

Groucho Marx said, 'I wouldn't want to belong to any club that would accept me as a member.' Professor John Barrow, astrophysicist, mathematician, philosopher, playwright and Christian applies what he calls 'The Groucho Marx Effect' to cosmology, where he suggests that 'A Universe simple enough to understand is too simple to produce a mind capable of understanding it.' Professor Barrow's paradox shows the gravity of Groucho's wit. A definition of reality may not yet, if ever, be achievable.

What I am saying is that it is possible that we have not evolved to the level where we can understand all that our ape's great brain finds. At each discovery, we may lag behind. The prospect-refuge-driven Quest is the savannah of the mind, drawing us willy-nilly towards what lies beyond. It is our signature, our stimulus, our spur; and our threat to survival.

Powsels and thrums.

I go to let the hens out before breakfast They tumble from their hut to drink. One scratches for a worm. And something glints in the scratching, catching the sun. I pick it up and hold it, a stone, a wonder, in my hand. I know what this is; and I am the first to know in the eight to ten thousand years since the last hand that held it. And that hand and mine just could be linked.

I lift the stone against the light. It is thin, translucent, honey-black and sharp; sharper than a surgeon's steel; and in it, as if in amber, a fossil, a frond of a creature from the sea.

Back at the house for breakfast, I spoon muesli with one hand, and with the other turn the shining thing. It fits my fingers.

Two strikes made it; broke it free; and trimmed it to perfect the edge. Eight to ten thousand years ago.

Someone brought it here. After the ice went, people walked from Europe, following the herds. The flint was in Yorkshire. It passed from hand to hand around camp fires, a chalky lump, until it reached where the garden is now. A blow hit the lump, and the honey-black shone.

The spur of land sits above the valley, with water on three sides, and well-drained soil; a good winter camp for hunter-gatherers, and a time for mending and making, telling stories, watching for the game to come down to drink. Then skinning the flesh of the kill.

The postman drives up the track into the yard. I slit the envelope. Inside is the result of the radiocarbon dating of a cremation we disturbed at the corner of the house. The figure 3,445 plus or minus 29 BP, which means three thousand five hundred years ago, give or take. The house stands on an Early Bronze Age barrow. And though the house is five hundred years old and more, it is not the first. There is at least one other beneath; with earlier roundhuts under the garden and the yard. The people that came here after the ice did not go away. Why move when you find the place ideal?

And what about the flint I am holding? How did that happen?

Sixty-six million years ago there was a warm sea over what is now England, and in it were plankton and snails. They died; and their scales and shells drifted down and settled on the sea floor. They built the chalk more than half a kilometre thick.

But a kilometre is a cold measure. I cannot relate to a length that is based on one ten-millionth of the distance from the equator to the pole. My mind is one of miles. A mile is a measure of the body; a pace, a fifteen-minute walk. It is the measure that brought us out of Africa with a stone in our hand.

The weight of half a mile of chalk pressed the silica of the shells and scales. Larger creatures burrowed through the ooze, and the silica followed, filling the tunnels and burrows; settled, and was hard, a cast of where they'd been.

The world heaved, the chalk weathered, and the silica became flint. Inside its grey husk it grew beauty, waiting to be got.

We walked out of Africa ninety thousand years ago. We came by flint. Flint makes and kills; gives shelter, food; it clothes us. Flint clears forest. Flint brings fire. With flint we bear the cold.

A heart-shaped pebble, worn by water, lies in a shallow brook. A hand takes it.

The pebble fits the hand. It's hard and black and good. But it can be better. It can be made better. The mind sees how; and the other hand strikes with another stone. It knocks flakes from one side of the black, each flake drawing sparks into a sharp and wavy edge. The point of the heart is pressed more gently to whittle slivers; and the work is done.

Now the pebble is an axe in the hand, to butcher with. The edge cuts hide and flesh and sinew and opens up the marrow of a bone. The point digs between and prises limbs apart.

What is this that is coming?

Mervyn stands by the belt on the tractor as the potatoes are lifted from the field. He picks off the rubbish. The tractor passes over the pond that the motorway men filled with their spoil when they made the cutting. The earth is claggy and yellow, not loam, and there are more stones than spuds. He throws the stones back to the field.

He takes one to sling; and stops. It's black, and it sits in his hand, just right. It's small and smooth, but jagged on one side and pointed at the end. The stone gleams, and there is light inside.

Mervyn puts the stone in his pocket, and on his way home he drops it off at the house on the hill.

I sit in the old house on the ancient mound and read the County Archaeologist's notes.

Site. A reclaimed marl-pit at Grid Reference SJ 777/744755 filled with spoil from a cutting on the M6.

Description. The artefact is a black pebble of

conchoidal fracture, with smooth, natural facets and naturally rounded butt, all showing derived features. The end has been pointed by pressure flaking, and on one side a sinuous edge has been formed by bifacial chipping and step-flaking to give a triangular section. The other side has been heavily blunted.

Remarks. On the superficial evidence, it would appear to be a Lower Palaeolithic handaxe, preserved from destruction under the Anglian and subsequent glaciations. It is Abbevillean in execution.

I sit back. Abbevillean. That's more than six ice ages ago. It must be half a million years. How did it survive?

Half a million. It wasn't *Homo sapiens*. *Homo erectus*, perhaps. Or *Homo heidelbergensis*. Or some such. And now in my hand.

I look out of the window at the telescope. The dish is tilted. The antenna is collecting signals so faint that they have to be cooled to near absolute zero to steady the radio waves before the data can be sent to the computers.

A light, not thought, flashes in my brain.

I log on to the telescope to find what it's hearing. It's a quasar, a mass of energy with a black hole at its centre; near the beginning of Time, more than thirteen thousand million light years away, more than thirteen thousand million years ago; before our solar system was formed; before our galaxy took shape. And the whispers of that energy, travelling at the speed of light, about one hundred and eighty thousand miles a second, seven times around the world in a second, one and a quarter seconds to the Moon, eight minutes to the Sun, four point two years to the nearest star, two point five million to the nearest galaxy like ours – the whispers are arriving at the antenna of the telescope Now; if Now exists; if Now is possible. And I sit with the axe in my hand. It is such a little thing.

The axe is a first meddling with the Universe by our intelligence. Intelligence took what was and changed it, to make it work better. Once that has happened, the telescope becomes inevitable. Idea leads to idea in a chain reaction of discovery that won't be stopped. Eve will pick the apple. Pandora cannot shut the box. We are the ape that asks, 'What's next?'

The pebble opens the Cosmos. If mind had not interfered with pebble, if hand had not struck flake, no dish would hear, and no antenna focus.

Half a million years. Thirteen thousand million years.

When the hand picked the pebble to fetch the telescope, the whispers had covered some 99 per cent of their journey to this Cheshire field. And I hold the stone, full of stars. And wonder.

The pebble opens the Cosmos. And yet, lost in the immensity of understanding, should I not fear this thing?

'Abbevillean in execution', says the note. The axe is named from the place where its type was first identified. Intelligence shaped it. But is intelligence enough to save us from ourselves? And are we, alone, intelligent in this vastitude? May it be that we have not yet found intelligence beyond our world because intelligence that evolves to be conscious of itself carries its own destruction within? Will the flint that shaped us be our nemesis, our nemesis of Abbevillean execution?

We have been to Abbeville more than once. We have had practice. We have rehearsed. Abbeville is in the valley of the Somme.

I accept the thought, and choose to ignore it; just as I accept and ignore that the Sun's future is finite. To do other would result in stasis and stagnation. It is enough that an ape, sitting on a wet rock orbiting an unremarkable star at the edge of an ordinary example of uncounted galaxies in one of perhaps an infinite number of universes, should have evolved to feel such wonder.

In this sense, though we may have valid personal faith, it is right that, for good or ill, we may never 'know', because then we should ccasc to ask. Which is why those that insist that they do 'know', the zealots of all kinds, secular or other, block progress. They are entrenched. They are refuge without prospect. They shut down creativity. They are atrophy. Fundamentalists do not question. They have stopped.

It has been said before.

Lord Vishnu sat on Mount Chomolungma, and wept.

Along comes Hanuman, the monkey god, and he says, 'What are you crying at? And what are all those ants down there shouting for?'

'They're not ants,' says Vishnu. 'They're people. I was holding the Jewel of Absolute Wisdom; and I dropped it; and it fell into the World and broke. Everybody has a splinter; but they each think they've got the whole thing, and they run around, screaming at each other; and no one listens.'

Through art we may glimpse some of the truth that we have been clever enough to feel, yet are not clever enough to understand. But we can learn. We can move. We can grow. Art complements science, and science art. They fuel each other's creativity, as they help us to ponder our being.

So I sit in the house on the mound and watch the telescope; pick, pluck, tease and weave the powsels and the thrums; and tell the stories; and take the risks.

I'd be a damn' fool if I didn't.

Water of life, water of death,
And the king asleep in the ground.

22

By Seven Firs and Goldenstone

Landscapes can be deceptive.

Sometimes a landscape can seem to be less a setting for the life of its inhabitants than a curtain behind which their struggles, achievements and accidents take place.

For those who, with the inhabitants, are behind the curtain, landmarks are no longer only geographic but biographical and personal.

John Berger, *A Fortunate Man*

A topographically significant landscape feature such as [the Edge] could easily have become connected with memories and ancestral associations of earlier genera-tions of hunter-gatherers, for whom the Edge could have formed an important landmark through which to navigate not only the physical landscape but also on which to fasten mythological meaning.

R. W. Cowell in 'The Archaeology of Alderley Edge', *British Archaeological Reports* (BAR 396), 2005, p. 32

Grandad told me this tale. He told it in the dark of his forge, and by the side of his hearth, and in his garden as we pulled rhubarb. He told it with simplicity, respect, authority; and he would not have brooked doubt. It was his truth, a part of him, which he passed on.

Here is how he told it. I have simplified his dialect; it is the manner of the telling that is important. And note how he uses the Present Tense, as if the story is still happening.

'There's a farmer living down Mobberley. And he has him a white mare. And he must take this mare to sell her at Macclesfield market.

So off he sets one day at the back end of October; and just as it's coming light he's crossing the Edge, but when he gets to Thieves' Hole, the mare stops and won't budge, choose what he does. Against the side of the road he sees a tall old chap, thin as a rasher of wind; and he's got a proper sort of a stick in his hand.

"Oh," he says, this chap, "that's just the mare I'm after. How much do you want for her?"

"I'm not selling to the likes of you," says farmer. "I'll get more at market."

"You go your ways," says the old chap. "You'll not sell her. And I'll be waiting for you tonight."

So off farmer rides to market. And he sits there all day; but though everybody says she's a grand beast, no one offers to buy that mare. And at the finish, he has to get him back to Mobberley with her.

When he comes to Thieves' Hole it's fetching night. And there's the old chap waiting for him.

"Now will you sell?" he says.

"How much will you give?" says farmer.

"Enough," he says. "You come with me."

And off he tramps, with farmer behind him.

They go from Thieves' Hole, by Seven Firs, and Goldenstone, to Stormy Point and Saddlebole. And on Saddlebole they come to a rock, big as our house nearly.

The old chap touches the rock with his stick, and the rock splits open, clatter. And behind the rock there's some iron gates. He touches them with his stick, and they open; and there's a rum sort of a hole going into the hill.

By this time farmer, he's asking the old chap to let him go, and keep the mare. He wants no money for her.

But the old chap tells him he'll not come to no harm, he says. So farmer takes the mare down into the hill, after him.

They come to a cave; and there, all around, are knights in armour and a big man with them, asleep with their heads each against a white horse, except one, and he has nobbut a ruck of stones for rest on.

"This here," says the old chap, "is a sleeping army, with their Top Man and their horses, waiting on the last battle of the world, and whenever that day is I must wake them. But I'm one horse short, and yours will do nicely. Now you come with me."

And he takes farmer to another cave; and this one is full of gold and silver and all sorts. "Have as much as you can carry," he says, "and we'll call that payment."

Well, farmer, he sets to and he crams his boots and his pockets, his britches and his shirt with the treasure; and his hat; and when he can hold no more, the old chap takes him back to the iron gates and shoves him through. Another clatter and a bang, and when farmer turns him round, there's just the rock and it's black as a bag outside.

Well, farmer, he gets home as best he may and tells his tale; and the next morning him and his neighbours they go back to the Edge to fetch more treasure; but neither they nor any since have seen the iron gates again.'

That is the tale Grandad told. It is the Legend of Alderley. What Grandad did not know, and would not have cared if he had, is that the Legend, in various forms, occurs across at least the northern hemisphere, at all times and in many places. It is the myth of the Sleeping Hero. Aspects of it are in the earliest written record of any myth, *The Epic of Gilgamesh*, baked on clay tablets, some dating from the second millennium BC. Incidents differ, but at their most simple and comprehensive the stories involve the encounter of a mortal, through an intermediary, with an immortal, asleep under the ground in a special or sacred place.

Here, it is necessary to say what is meant by a legend in the study of folklore. The technical definition of a legend is: 'A fanciful story associated with a place and believed to be true by the people that live there.' I remember, as a child during World War II, listening to adults joking, yet only half joking, and nervously, that if the knights were ever going to wake now was the time;

but they would need white tanks not white horses. The story was fulfilling its definition of a legend.

The clearest statement is that of K. M. Briggs. '[Folk Tale] is Folk Fiction, told for edification, delight or amusement. Folk Legend was once believed to be true . . . A difficulty arises when [legends] are handed on by people who no longer believe them, for entertainment or as curiosities. Then they begin to be embellished with picturesque touches, new circumstances, and the legend becomes a fiction.' More poetically, but no less cogently, John Maruskin writes: 'It is in the speech of carters and housewives, in the speech of blacksmiths and old women, that one discovers the magic that sings the claim of the voice in the shadow, or that chants the rhyme of the fish in the well.'

Both writers' words are exemplified by the early printed texts of the Legend. The first, recorded in the *Manchester Mail* in May 1805, is dull; the second is a bolted lettuce of verbiage, an example of how to make polite literature from the vulgar. It is nothing else.

'[The farmer] perceived a figure before him, of more than common height, clad in a sable vest, which enveloped his figure; over his head he wore a cowl, which bent over his ghastly visage, and screened not hid, the eyes, that sunken and scowling, were now fully bent upon the horseman; in his hand he held a staff of black wood, this he extended so as to prevent the horse from proceeding until he had addressed the rider. When he essayed to speak his countenance became more spectre-like, and in a hollow yet commanding voice, he said, "Listen, Cestrian! I know thee, whence thou comest, and what is thy errand to yonder fair! That errand shall be fruitless; thy steed is destined to fulfil a nobler fate . . .'"

Compare it with Grandad's delivery.

The different forms of the theme have been much discussed. It is primarily a version of the near-universal motif of the Sleeping Hero – the Saviour that must never wake, since he represents the last hope of his people. He is the ace in the hand; and once that is played there is nothing left to hope for. In the versions where he is disturbed by a mortal he asks, 'Is it yet Time?' And the mortal answers, 'No. Sleep you on.'

This element of partial waking is not found in the Legend of Alderley. It is more pertinent that the Greek historian Plutarch, in his book *Concerning the Failure of Oracles*, written in the first century AD, quotes the report of Dimitrios, who had been sent by the Emperor of Rome to gather information about the islands of Britain. 'There is, men said, an island in which Kronos is imprisoned with Briareus keeping guard over him as he sleeps. For, as they put it, Sleep is the bond forged for Kronos. They add that around him are many divine beings, his knights and his soldiers.'

Plutarch was using names that Romans and Greeks would recognise. What their British equivalents were we can only guess, but the names of individuals appear not to be important. In the Legend of Alderley, the old man is not at first called a wizard, and his name of Merlin and that of Arthur for the Sleeping Hero are nineteenth-century decorations. In the Legend as it was told to me, they were simply an 'old chap' and a 'Top Man'.

I am not suggesting that Plutarch is referring to Alderley. There are at least eight versions of the Legend in the British Isles. What I am saying is that the story existed in this part of Europe in the Iron Age; and a question is: why should it occur on the Edge? An answer is: I do not know.

A bigger question would be how and why the legends, different yet the same, should have spread so far through space and time. But the Edge has enough of its own to challenge us. Why, when and how did the story start its journey to me through Grandad's mouth and the mouths of others of the Edge?

The most reliable source to trace is oral, for the reasons given. The difference between the oral and the written is that the written is a fiction, whereas the oral, however changed, is, in its origin, an attempt to retain, perhaps to explain, a reality. It is news that time has warped: a game of Chinese Whispers passed from generation to generation, until the meaning may be lost, but the elements remain. How may we find them?

By the time I was eighteen I had learnt an important rule of research: Pursue the Anomaly. If something does not make sense, what is it saying? And there are anomalies in the truth Grandad told me about the land he knew best.

The most obvious one is that no farmer in his right mind would take a horse twelve miles over rough ground, involving a climb of some four hundred feet, to get to Macclesfield, when, by waiting a week, he could have sold it at Knutsford, three miles away across the flat.

But here is the anomaly that concerns us most.

In the Legend the old man stops the farmer at a place called Thieves' Hole. To get from there to the spot where the old man opens the way to the cavern, at a rock known as the Iron Gates, the farmer is led by an unnecessary route: 'from Thieves' Hole, by Seven Firs, and Goldenstone, to Stormy Point and Saddlebole'.

Until the eighteenth century the Edge was an unenclosed, all but treeless 'dreary common'. The woods that we see now are the result of deliberate landscaping. Why, then, did the old man traipse the farmer across an open hillside in a zigzag that increased the journey by more than 20 per cent? What 'truth' was my grandfather remembering about the land he knew best?

I went to look for the Why and the What. And in trying to answer these questions I set out on a journey: a journey no less mysterious than the farmer's. It was a journey into the land, and the land was itself the telling of a story, the narration of a tale that followed a path and took its line from waymarkers, just as the Legend does.

At each of the named places on the route from Thieves' Hole to the Iron Gates I found interferences with the ground, in the form of earthworks, big stones, and, above all, ancient boundaries. I was confronted by something old, possibly prehistoric.

The places were important to Grandad, and, even though he did not know the exact position of every one, the route was beyond doubt, and a search filled in the gaps. And since place names in England tend to be among the earliest survivors from the past, when names were descriptive only (and that is important), identifying what was then seen as fact, here was where to start to look for a clew through the temporal and physical maze. I began to question the names.

Most place-name elements in Cheshire are Old English (the language of the Anglo-Saxons), Old Norse, Middle English or Old French in origin. That is, they were in the language by the end of the fourteenth century, at least in speech. They may turn up later in documents, but the document does not date the name. It records what exists.

The old man stopped the farmer at Thieves' Hole. Old English *hol* means 'valley', 'depression', or in describing roads, 'sunken'. Middle English *þeof* is 'thief'. In modern Cheshire speech, 'hole' is qualified by an adjective, as in 'mine hole', 'sand hole', 'pit hole'. The Old English *pytt* is an excavated hole, where minerals or other materials are got. An example of this is the quarry in a larger depression below Bradford Lodge on the north side of Bradford Lane, known as Stonpit Hole (stone pit hole), which distinguishes between the two elements. (OS. SJ 845 768)

Were it not for etymology and usage, the 'hole' of Thieves' Hole would be the small quarry close by; but that is not a 'hole'. It is a 'pit'. The 'hole' passes under a farm road as a double sunken depression.

Thieves' Hole could be both a road and a boundary; they are often one and the same. It is not a boundary of any existing land division at this point now, but it could have been used as such, whatever its original purpose, in the early Middle Ages for an estate now lost.

A charter of 1008 for Rolleston, Staffordshire, describes one of the boundary marks as *ðan þorne þer ða þeofes licgað*, 'to the thorn where the thieves lie'. And at Witney, Oxfordshire, in 1044, there occurs *Of Æcenes felda ðær ða cnitas licgað*, 'From Æcen's field where the lads lie'. The Old English verb *licgan* means 'to lie', not in wait but as a corpse. It indicates a place of execution and/or burial; and for this the Anglo-Saxons came to favour boundaries. It was not so at first. To begin with, the Anglo-Saxons' approach had more of the numinous than of dread. But with the introduction of Christianity there was a movement from pagan respect for the ancient to a God-goaded fear.

Thieves' Hole as a place name occurs four more times in Cheshire alone. In the township of Fallibroome, next to Alderley, it is the name of a field that lies between the confluence of two brooks, each arm of which forms the boundary with Prestbury. Three more occur in Hattersley, along the banks of the river Mersey, the meaning of which is 'boundary water'.

From Thieves' Hole, by Seven Firs, and Goldenstone,
to Stormy Point and Saddlebole.

One of the enigmas of the Edge is the occurrence of artificial, flat-topped mounds of earth of no known age or purpose. They could be prehistoric burials; they could be more recent 'improvements' for the romanticisation of the new woodland; they could be both, or almost anything. With one exception, they have no name, but the route from Thieves' Hole to Saddlebole takes in three of them, including the one exception, which is called Seven Firs. Only excavation would answer the question of what these circular features are, but a geophysical survey of Seven Firs has shown seven 'anomalies' in the mound, which could be the remains of tree roots. All over the country, especially in the eighteenth century, it was common for landscapes to be 'improved' aesthetically by the planting of clumps on old bumps.

From Thieves' Hole, by Seven Firs, and Goldenstone, to Stormy Point and Saddlebole.

The earliest surviving mention of Goldenstone is in a Perambulation of the boundary between Over Alderley and Nether Alderley of 1598: '. . . and so to a great stone called the golden stone on the north side of the wain way . . .'

Goldenstone, which marks a kink in the parish boundary, has the appearance of age and a mixed history. It is a freestanding irregular but worked block of conglomerate sandstone, notable for its high content of quartz pebbles. It seems to have been shaped by battering; that is, not with metal tools. And it is not golden, it is grey. It has been badly used, in that a portion has been destroyed, and the traces of drill holes that remain suggest the use of explosives. But the rock has no useful purpose, and there is the finest freestone close by. At a comparatively recent date, within the past few centuries, someone tried to obliterate it. An earth bank covered it, and I exposed it again in 1955.

When complete, Goldenstone weighed about twelve tons and was hauled into place from some distance when there was plenty of other stone that would have served the purpose nearby. This, together with the nature of its tooling, is consistent with a prehistoric origin for its placement. But why is a grey stone called 'golden'?

There are many 'golden stones' in England. We need to look at language again.

In place names, Old English *gylden* can mean several things. 1) 'Gold-coloured': plainly not the case here. 2) 'Sacrifice'. 3) 'Tribute, tax'. 4) 'Treasure'. 5) 'Wealthy'. 6) 'Splendid'. It is a matter of choice, unless other evidence turns up. I intuitively reject 'sacrifice', and tend towards 'tribute'. A boundary is neutral, neither here nor there, a good symbolic place for the safe transfer of wealth, since, while it is on the boundary, the tribute is nowhere and can belong to no one. Behind Goldenstone is the second flat-topped mound.

From Thieves' Hole, by Seven Firs, and Goldenstone, to Stormy Point and Saddlebole.

The route from Goldenstone to Stormy Point follows the boundary between Over Alderley and Nether Alderley. As it reaches Stormy Point it passes by the third flat-topped mound.

Old English *stormig* is 'stormy'. Middle English, from Old French, *pointe* is 'a place having definite spatial position, but no extent, or of which the position alone is considered; a spot'. This may be convoluted, but it is an accurate description of Stormy Point; and there is much to note on its amorphous ground.

For the present purpose, there is the Devil's Grave: a

small discoidal chamber entered by an open trench that runs along one side. In form it is unique on the Edge, unless it is the same type of working of which traces may be seen at Engine Vein, but almost destroyed there by the later cutting. 'Devil' is used frequently in the naming of strangeness, especially of early features in the landscape. The sense is that they are 'other': unsafe things from long ago and a different kind of time. Also, naming and renaming matters where places or things are already recognised, have meaning, and need to be dealt with; which is often done by demonisation of prehistoric remains at the time of conversion from paganism to Christianity. Old English *græf* is, essentially, 'something dug in stone: a cave, or a trench'. Again the description is apt: 'the tricky trench'.

Close by the Devil's Grave is a now inconspicuous circular mound: Pikelow. Old English *piced*, 'pointed', and Old English *hlāw*, 'mound', and, well attested as the most common meaning, 'artificial mound', 'burial mound', 'barrow'. What makes Pikelow significant beyond its appearance is that the boundaries of three parishes and four townships meet at its centre.

Boundaries, of great age in themselves, when first defined often used visible, well-known aspects of the landscape as reference points. Natural features are common, as are pre-existing artificial ones, and also isolated trees. It is likely that Goldenstone was used because it was already there. Similarly, Pikelow was not built to be used as a boundary marker but was chosen because it was of importance and beyond dispute. The boundary was strung between.

From Thieves' Hole by Seven Firs, and Goldenstone, to
Stormy Point and Saddlebole.

We, and the farmer, are on the last leg of the journey; and it is the most intriguing one.

Saddlebole is a spur from Stormy Point, with a dip the shape of a saddle about halfway along its length. The further summit ridge ends in a steep convex slope. Old English *sadol*. Old English *bol*, 'a smooth, rounded hill'.

There is another meaning for *bole* that may apply to this part of the Edge, where copper and lead have been worked from early periods, and amounts of iron, cobalt, manganese, sulphur, silver, mercury and tin occur. Old English *bolla* is 'a round hollow', 'a bowl', 'a crucible'.

Bole, as a mining term, is first found in print in *Fodinæ Regales, or the History, Laws and Places of the Chief Mines and Mineral Works in England, Wales, and the English Pale in Ireland, as also of the Mint and Mony. With A CLAVIS Explaining some difficult Words relating to Mines, &c. By Sir John Pettus, Knight. 1670.*

Sir John was deputy governor of the royal mines, and his book was the standard treatise of the seventeenth century. In the clavis, there is the entry: 'Boles or Bolestids are places where in ancient time, before Smelting Mills were invented, the Miners did fine their lead.'

The spur of Saddlebole begins at Stormy Point. A preliminary excavation here in 2007 produced lead scoriae and other smelting waste, together with broken lumps of unburnt lead ore, galena. Future work will show whether or not boles are present. Certainly this part of the hill would suggest that they are. The concentration of metals in the soil here prohibits any kind of vegetation.

Saddlebole may have had an importance that anachronistic modern thought would miss. The *Fodinæ* is concerned not only with metallurgy but also with alchemy, and it should be remembered that the division between the two was once more permeable than it is today. Saddlebole may have been associated with a Mystery, to add to its other, ancient, otherness.

At the side of the track, which is another multiple boundary, descending from Stormy Point to the saddle, there is the dramatic rock of the Iron Gates. I have not seen the name identified as being that rock in any written or printed form. How, then, do I know that it is the Iron Gates of the Legend, the way to the Sleeping Hero? Grandad told me. And how did he know? Someone told him; as they too had been told. Question or proof did not come into it.

Remember that we are dealing with legend, and legend is belief of truth. It is not fiction. It is not imagination. It is not invention. It is reportage. But why the Iron Gates? A solid rock should not need an iron gate.

In European legend, folklore and mythology, iron gates commonly occur as entrances to the Land of the Dead. These gates are found not so much in the depths of the earth as in hills and rocks that rise above the level ground. They are opened sometimes by touching them with a particular flower, but more often what translates as a 'wishing rod' is used, although there are other names, such as 'fire rod', 'burn rod', 'burst rod', and 'quake rod'. Descriptions of it vary, but it is most commonly a single, slender staff, the same as the 'proper sort of a stick' that the 'old chap' uses on the Edge.

So much for the zigzag journey. Yet there are questions to be asked of the Legend from the start.

Why was it that the old man stopped the farmer at Thieves' Hole? And what was a farmer travelling from Mobberley doing there in the first place? He could not have been on any modern road.

The double ditch has been interpreted as the 'braiding' of an ancient hollow way running from the north-west to the south-east along the ridge of the Edge and possibly prehistoric in origin. Beyond Thieves' Hole, in the right conditions, the track may be seen as a crop mark heading towards The Black Greyhound, from where there is a choice of roads to Macclesfield.

In the other direction, the track has been traced to the A34 opposite Alderley Cottage. It does not end there. The line continues, with the immediate surface detail lost or obscured, across the A34, along the side of the house and down to join Cuttlers (now Lydiat) Lane, from which it is visible as a hollow way in the lower part of the garden and as far as the hedge of the lane. (OS. SJ 84273 77956)

From there, with a little jinking over the railway, paths and boundaries lead to and through Common Carr farm (its track an Urban District boundary and the find spot of a Bronze Age palstave) to the B5085, which is the southern fringe of the ritual waters of Lindow Moss (with its Lindow Men); and so to Mobberley. But why is Mobberley a part of the Legend?

Back at Thieves' Hole, we still have to cope with the old man. Why did he stop the mare here?

Today a farm road crosses the double ditch at right angles on its way from the B5087 to Edge House. It is along this road that the zigzag journey starts. On the earliest surviving Stanley Estate Map of 1787 no road is shown. However, when dealing with cartography, we need to know what information the commissioner of the map wanted or needed to record. Only with the appearance of the Ordnance Survey's discipline is accuracy mandatory. Earlier, absence of evidence is not evidence of absence.

It is plausible to suppose that the 'missing' road was there, perhaps a little off its present course, before 1787. To the south and north of the hiatus there are tracks, running in part along hollow ways, and they line up to cross the Edge at Thieves' Hole. It does not make sense for two track systems, approaching each other head on, to stop. But I may be pernickety. The tracks are climbing to open common and heath. Once there the ways would not be so confined, and what the Legend implies may be more accurately described as movement between known and named points.

If the various tracks do continue and cross over Thieves' Hole they should be the later feature. But roads are deceptive, in that their function alters through time, which causes changes in size and surface. In the archaeology of landscape, tarmac is the great deceiver of the eye. To determine what, if any, relationship may exist between the two ways their intersection would have to be excavated. Should there be a true relationship and intersection, then Thieves' Hole would have formed a crossroad; and crossroads share the uncertainty and the uncanny with boundaries, for the same reason: they are ambivalent. The centre of a crossroad leads nowhere, just as the centre of Pikelow, with its joined seven boundaries, occupies nowhere. Such liminal places are where space and time are weakened and other dimensions may break through. That is why, I suggest, boundaries play so great a part in the Legend.

I go further and say that if a crossroad did not exist at Thieves' Hole the old man would not have met the farmer there. And to find the place now would require the disciplines of archaeology and folklore working together.

We, with our modern, materialistic minds, think of time and space linearly: that is, yesterday-today-tomorrow time, and behind-here-before-up-down space. With these views we form only a small part of human thought. The majority of the world, including many of the great religions, preliterate cultures, physicists and cosmologists (and these only as an example), have no difficulty in accepting multiple realities, which I shall call 'mythic' space and time.

'Myth' is an abused word, equated with 'untruth', whereas it is the opposite. At our most profound, we can never say what we mean. The mirror that reflects meaning is metaphor and poetry, but what they reflect is truth. By 'myth' I do not imply 'fiction', but more the weaving of patterns that we unconsciously recognise as the core of being, both within and without us. Myth is as near as words, through poetry and metaphor, can get to the wholeness of perfect truth.

In the Legend we are dealing with physical and spiritual mythic topography. Boundaries and centres are a large part of the structure. They are 'betwixts-and-betweens', midpoints or the midway line between opposites; neither this nor that. The dividing lines without breadth symbolise the supernatural in the realm of space. Temporally, the same phenomenon is represented as the juncture between years, seasons, days: 'today' (which never was and never will be, and yet is). Both kinds of line are occupied by a mysterious power, which has a propensity both for good and evil. This supernatural power, when applied to time, breaks through in a most ominous way on November Eve and May Eve in 'Celtic', that is Iron Age, culture. They are the joints between the two great seasons of the year.

November Eve, called *Samhain* in Ireland, the start of winter and of the year, was a solemn and weird festival. The mounds were open and their inhabitants were abroad in a more real sense than on any other night. The boundary between the living and the dead was breached.

And which temporal boundary is 'at the back end of October', when the farmer goes out of his world to meet the Sleeping Hero? Consider, too, how the first meeting with the old man is at the boundary between night and day, dawn, and the second at dusk.

Boundaries between territories, like boundaries between times, are lines along which the supernatural intrudes through the surface of existence. The union of two opposites is symbolised by the line along which they impinge upon one another; and the reconciliation of three or more independent entities involves the discovery of the point at which they coincide.

The Legend speaks philosophy as story. It is why the old man has to meet the farmer at a crossroad, a road without direction or commitment, at a time when time is stopped. Once the farmer turns from his way home, he is entering another reality. The approach to the Sleeping Hero begins with the first step from Thieves' Hole, and with each step the farmer moves out of his reality into another, to return for ever changed.

Surveys of physical boundaries are themselves often enigmatic. It is by no means easy to follow the Perambulation of 1598.

'. . . And so lineally to a little mere-stone in the track way towards the mineholes and so to the mere-stone at the top of the hill and from thence on the north side [of] the minehole directly to the Saddlebole and so from the Saddlebole along under the great stones after the crest. And so back after the crest by the great stones to the two stones lying together over against the hanging stone on the slack . . .' The cause of confusion may be the combination of different factors, not least that the document is of its moment and not of ours, when the people concerned knew what was being referred to. They knew; but often knowledge has been lost, so that we have to look at the ground carefully, and sometimes guess. A particular hazard is the interpretation of individual names. The misunderstanding of a single letter or syllable can alter meaning. It may stretch belief that 'oaks at the wolf's green' could ever have been claimed as 'sandy ridge of the elves' or 'green ridge of the elf', but I once claimed it, and with reason, though that reasoning was wrong. I shall try to make more rigorous sense here, because there is the chance that something important is lurking in the word thicket.

The boundary on Saddlebole is intriguing, not least for its being the earliest documented description of the topography of a part of the Edge.

It is a record, written in Medieval Contracted Latin, of a grant of land dating from the thirteenth century. The text is corrupted in its printing.

Walking the land, I read the text as: 'Greetings. I, John of Arderne, lord of Alderley, gave and bequeathed to John, son of Edmund Fyton, and to his heirs all my land with the wood rising above the aforesaid land within these divisions; namely: taking to Elfgrenhoks by rising as far as the Sadel and from the Sadel following the one-time road as far as the Birchenegros and to the Pykedlowe and from the Pykedlowe and so on to Avardeshache and from there to Fitton's hunting station, and so on.'

The meaning of the marker names on Saddlebole would appear to be: Elfgrenhocks: 'Oaks at the wolf green'; Old English, *wulf*, 'wolf'; Old English *grēne*, 'a grassy place'; Old English *ac*, 'oak'. If the definition is accurate, Elfgrenhocks may still exist. On the line of the boundary there is a single oak, and single oaks were often boundary markers. It could be the oldest tree on the Edge, since it attained its shape by growing at a time when there was no competition. It grew on the 'dreary common'. I am not claiming that the oak is eight hundred years old, though that is not impossible, but I do argue that it is in a place where an oak would have been handy; so it may be a replacement. Sadel: 'Saddle'. Birchenegros: 'Birch grove'; Old English, *birchen*, 'birchen'; Old English *grāf*, 'copse'. Pykedlowe: 'Pikelow'. Avardeshache: 'Ælfweard's gate'; Old English personal name: *Ælfweard*; Old English *hæc*, 'gate'. Fytounes trystre: 'Fitton's hunting station'; Middle English personal name: *Fytoune*; Middle English *trystre*, 'hunting station'.

'Ælfweard' is a personal name, but it breaks down into two elements: Old English *ælf*, 'elf' (and in the Saxon period an elf was no whimsy but a spiritual force, even carrying the meaning of 'god'); and Old English *weard*, 'ward'. I felt that this was too important a matter to risk, so I asked Ralph Elliott. Here is his reply.

'Auardeshacche/Avardeshache. Your suggestion that this is not Ælfweard's gate, but the elf-guard's gate is perfectly possible. In the West Midlands the words "elf, elves" are recorded as "alve, alven", according to the *Middle English Dictionary*, Part E. 1, p. 72. These words occur several times in Layamon's *Brut*, c. AD 1200 according to C. S. Lewis's Introduction to G. L. Brook's edition. Thus "the gate of the elf-guard" is a good West Midland reading, perfect for Alderley!'

The Sleeping Hero could be called an elf in this context; and the old man his ward, a 'god-guard'.

Boundaries can be among the longest-surviving of our monuments. Many delineate Saxon estates, Roman and Iron Age structures, Bronze Age field systems, and a few even the Neolithic; and some can be combined in the one feature. However, the majority of our old boundaries are of Saxon origin. The Anglo-Saxons developed an ambivalent attitude towards these spaceless spaces, as has been noted. They feared them, and yet employed them because of their liminality for such purposes as execution sites and for the safe disposal of 'deviants'. These negative associations came with Christianity. Earlier, they were in awe of monuments, especially of Bronze Age round barrows, which they took as marker points for the boundaries of their land divisions, intensifying that liminal force, and they re-used the barrows, inserting their dead into the realm of the more ancient. Even natural features that looked like barrows were used. Yet these places, dangerous because of their lack of contact with the world while yet defining it, and unknown to God, were chosen as meeting places for assemblies both political and social, perhaps for that very neutrality, where disputes of this world held no sway. Mobberley, which means 'the mound of the assembly', has its church sited on an artificial circular earthwork, which may be the eponymous mound. From it the Beacon barrow mound on the Edge, skirted by the prehistoric road to Thieves' Hole, would have been visible. If there was a connection between the Edge and the mound of Mobberley, has folk memory preserved it as the route taken by the farmer? And what connection could there have been? I suggest that the link between mounds, moss and hill point to a landscape of the sacred, and that the Legend records it.

The swing of beliefs increased the Anglo-Saxons' association of ancient burials and boundaries with the uncanny. The no-places became synonymous with the supernatural. It is clear in the earliest surviving English epic, *Beowulf*, which dates from an uncertain time, possibly the seventh or eighth centuries. The poem is written from a Christian viewpoint, but its material is pagan.

Beowulf is a tale driven by boundaries and barrows. It contains the spatial topography understood by an eighth-century mind. Beowulf's first heroic victory is the killing of the monster Grendel, whose epithet is *mearc-stappa*, 'boundary-walker'; and his last victory, and his death, is in battle with a dragon from a mound. On boundaries and in barrows evil was confined until darkness dissolved the barriers from view.

Barrows, in tradition and in reality, could hold treasure, nowadays called 'grave goods', and the finding of them during secondary use of the barrow would give an extra bond with the past and add to the otherworldliness of the site. Here, by coincidence, yet not wholly coincidence, *Beowulf* and the Legend overlap. It is a part of the pattern of folklore to associate hollow hills, either natural or artificial, with the other world and with riches. It is as if the image were hardwired into our psyches. In *Beowulf* the dragon is guarding a treasure in the mound.

> *Hord beweotode,*
> *Stānbeorh stēapne;　stīg under læg*
> *Eldum uncūð.*

(ll.2212–14)

> It watched over the hoard,
> in a stone-roofed barrow.　Men did not know the way
> to it under the ground.

In the poem, a man discovers the hidden entrance and takes a goblet from the treasure. The comparison with the Mobberley farmer of the Legend is close.

Accounting for the Edge is not easy. The hill has been used since the end of the latest Ice Age, about ten thousand years ago. Worked flint is found there. But the culture of the Mesolithic could not be expected to leave other traces. However, by the age of twenty-one I felt that the Legend of Alderley, as told by Grandad, contained, as it were, a guide to an unrecognised Early Bronze Age, four thousand years ago. I was nearly sixty before persistence won through and made the archaeologists look; which justified both Grandad and Legend. Metal mining on the Edge has been radiocarbon dated to nearly four thousand years ago.

I would say that the Edge, crisscrossed with boundaries and earthworks, is itself liminal, a special, a holy, or a haunted place, dependent upon the historical moment of the viewer. It is a remarkable hill that was largely heath, another form of boundary, another no-man's-land, which stands out both from the plain and from the high ground to the east. And the nature and colours of its rock formations are striking. Such things would have been important at many levels of consciousness in earlier times, as they are, if to a lesser extent, today.

It may be that the Edge was first seen as a place of numen millennia before copper was worked here. Metallurgy has always been a magical and dangerous art, and its practitioners are magical and dangerous men. (Who else but the rightful king could draw the sword from the stone?) Yet before and after copper the Edge could have been valued and even revered more as a source of pigments for the decoration of the human body. Such practices are universal in space and time. Pigments were traded over distances, and their source was considered to be a place of power, a seat of spirituality. We, as children of the Edge, knew where to find our body paint: the green, the red, the blue, the yellow, the white, the black; and how to mix them in a paste of precious lard and dripping stolen from our mothers' jars in World War II. John Hockenhull, the mildest of boys, when daubed became a god. It would be interesting if the question of the source of the amount of copper found in the Iron Age bog bodies known as Lindow II and III, near Mobberley, could be resolved.

There is more in the Legend, when we listen: another question.

If some supernatural agency has gone to the trouble of creating a cavern to house an enchanted army against the day of ultimate trial, why is there the logistical error of being one horse short? Did no one count? And why is that required horse a mare?

Mares were not used in battle. Stallions were. Why is there a milk-white mare on the Edge? What is it the Sleeping Hero lacks? What is the need? I knew that I knew. But what? Then I remembered Giraldus Cambrensis.

Giraldus was a Welsh monk writing in Latin in the late twelfth century. He starts Chapter 25 of the third part of his *History and Topography of Ireland*, which was intended, in part, to show the backwardness of the Irish, with these words: 'There are some things that, if the urgent demands of my account did not require it, shame would prevent their being described. But the severe discipline of history spares neither truth nor modesty.' He then relates a ritual alleged to be found in Donegal when a king assumes power.

There is in the northern and farther part of Ulster, namely in Kenelcunill, a certain people which is accustomed to appoint its king with a rite altogether outlandish and abominable. When the whole people of that land has been gathered together in one place, a white mare is brought forward into the middle of the assembly. He who is to be inaugurated, not as a chief, but as an outlaw, has bestial intercourse with her before all, professing himself to be a beast also. The mare is then killed immediately, cut up in pieces, and boiled in water. A bath is prepared for the man afterwards in the same water. He sits in the bath surrounded by all his people, and all, he and they, eat of the meat of the mare which is brought to them. He quaffs and drinks of the broth in which he is bathed, not in any cup, or using his hand, but just dipping his mouth into it round about him. When this unrighteous rite has been carried out, his kingship and dominion have been conferred.

Giraldus is scandalised. But he is describing a profound religious act. Here, the mare is the complement of the king's strength, the receptacle of his power. The act is a new Creation, a cleansing, a Eucharist, and a sacrament.

Yet can the ceremony be a survival spanning three millennia to Giraldus? I see no reason to reject the thought. Using a rough rule of thumb, the period represents about 120 generations; that is, 120 tellers, 120 rememberers. It is our ability to read that inhibits our capacity for retention.

Support for the argument for a Bronze Age survival in

Ireland and, by inference, in the Legend, comes from Scandinavia. At Bohuslän, in Sweden, there is Bronze Age rock art that depicts the copulation that Giraldus describes, which resolves the anomaly of the 'missing' horse in the Legend of Alderley with exuberant and explicit vigour.

The same Bronze Age iconography is found at Valcamonica in Alpine Italy.

But if only there were written accounts dating from the Bronze Age, my instinct, I felt, would stand on firmer ground.

Then, at a moment without thought, I saw. The vision unrolled. There *are* written sources dating from the Bronze Age, which complement and expand the oral fragments in preliterate societies. I was looking at the rite of the Indo-European horse sacrifice.

Current opinion is that the Indo-European peoples and their cognate languages originated in the Yamnaya and related cultures on the plains of the Eurasian Steppe, where the horse was first domesticated in about 3500 BC, and spread to Northern India, the Near East, and Ireland. It was the domestication of the horse that enabled people, trade, ideas, stories, disease and war to travel faster and further, and, with the invention of the two-wheeled chariot, which was a platform for the rapid deployment of military strength, to overcome resistance in battle. This combination of intelligence, speed and stamina produced in effect a new animal. It may be that the mythical half-man half-horse Centaur has its origins here.

I turned to the Indian sacred texts, the Upanishads and the Vedas, some of the most ancient books in the world, dating from about 500 BC to 1500 BC, and derived from earlier oral sources. The horse, its cosmic importance, its sacrifice and sexual coupling with royalty, were present throughout.

The earliest Upanishad, *Brihadaranyaka*, starts with the words: 'The head of the sacrificed horse is the dawn; its sight is the sun; its breath is the wind.' The Rig Veda has: 'Let this horse bring us good cattle and good horses, male children and all kind of nourishing wealth . . . Let the horse with our offerings achieve sovereign power' (Hymn 1.162). And so on.

In all the texts the horse, predominantly white, is identified with a creator, sometimes the Sun, sometimes death (for death is a form of creation). And the sacrifice was reserved for royalty, the purpose being fertility, the conferring of sovereignty, the bringing about of the future and of the good of the people. Whether it be Donegal, the Indus Valley or Alderley, the pattern was the same. Even Imperial Rome sacrificed its October Horse.

I set out on a journey to find why Grandad told me a story, and I have told that journey as a story. As with the farmer, it has been a long way to market. I found my answer in the land, because the land itself is a narrative, paths and waymarkers its stories. The reworking of oral tradition and the reworking of landscape go hand in hand; and the mare and the man are one.

Is it all coincidence? I think not. In the dark of his forge, I heard from the lips of my grandfather traces of the Upanishads, the Rig Veda, Giraldus Cambrensis; even, perhaps, of *Gilgamesh*.

A story holding fragments of timelessness, archaeological

and spiritual truths, passed down in the memories of unlettered minds, the importance, if not the meaning, retained faithfully over four thousand years, was told to a child.

And here Grandad and Eric James meet. One gave an inheritance, the other the ways to know it. Together they shaped me.

There's that many indispensable folk in this world every graveyard's full of them.

23

Funeral in The Hough

A stroke killed Grandad in January 1955, his eightieth year. He did not die at once. He was put in his chair next to the fire, beneath the corner cupboard. One side of his face was the man I loved. The other had melted.

Later he was taken upstairs, and the death watch began.

The ceiling was pitched and low, so that we stood around him, sons and grandsons, no women, forced to lean over the bed.

At the end, his eldest son said, 'How many sustificates do we need?' The family had each other insured with the Macclesfield Co-operative Society. Grandad opened the eye on the living side and spoke his last words. 'I'm not going afore I'm ready.' The eye shut; and, until the sure signs of death showed, no one dared to speak.

The men went downstairs to broach the whisky, and the women, the wives, took over.

The talk in the room below was eulogy, and memory of what had made a life: how many horseshoes he had hammered out during the Great War; how he had wound the clock of the Big Chapel in the village every Monday morning at ten o'clock through five decades and more; how he had ridden his bicycle the measured mile between home and forge, almost enough to encircle the world twice at the equator; how he had played the E-flat cornet in The Hough Fizzers; how he had won the first-prize gold medal for the Best Cottage Garden of 1901; and questions about who should have the medal now.

The women were done, and we went to view him.

He lay, a white linen bandage across the top of his head and under his chin, holding his jaw, and cotton wool was in his nostrils. His nose was pointed, as it had never been in life; but the skew was gone from his face. It was young, in a way I had not known.

We walked through the dark the measured mile to our own beds. My father fell into a hedge.

The undertaker was wheelwright John Jennings, and Arthur Buckley made the coffin. Grandad had made and fitted many an iron tyre for them. Now they were fitting him.

On the day of the funeral we met in the house. Old men, relatives, who appeared only at funerals, sat around and spoke softly. They all had blue eyes and silver hair.

Mosscrop's hearse drew up with Grandad in his coffin, and behind him the cars. We left the house, down the path to the gate and took our seats. The cortège moved off. The women stayed.

The Hough Chapel, which Grandad's grandad had helped to build, was two hundred yards away. We could have walked, but we were driven at a slower pace than walking, and no one spoke.

At the Chapel we formed up according to age, rank and

blood, and went in. The coffin was put on a trestle at the far end while the congregation of our people stood: Allmans, Baguleys, Fords, Hamnets, Leahs, Philipses, Sumners, Woolams; the community of The Hough. We sang 'Rock of Ages', and sat down on the benches. The Minister spoke, but we did not hear him. The Minister was ever a stranger, who moved on after three years; while we stayed. We had said all that Joseph Garner needed. Then it was 'Abide with Me' and out to the cars.

I sat in the front seat of the front car and was the nearest to Grandad. We set off for the cemetery, a mile and a half away on the other side of the village. Now the cortège did not creep, but went as fast as Mosscrop's could make it go. I watched the coffin tilt and bounce and slide all the way to the entrance arch of the cemetery, where we stopped, and crept again.

The cemetery was divided by an avenue. On the right was Church of England; and on the left was Methodist; and in a corner, overgrown with evergreens, were 'Suicides and Other Faiths'.

We lined up short of the grave, so that Joseph could be seen to be carried by his own. The four sons should have been the bearers, but Richard was too short and was asthmatic. A compromise of kin was needed. The coffin bit into my shoulder. He had not been so heavy in life.

We carried him to the grave, an east wind and sleet in our faces. The grave was edged with green raffia to mask the absolute. We eased him onto baulks of wood that spanned the trench and John Jennings gave us each a rope to hold. The baulks were pulled away and we lowered him. The rope fed through my hands, the weight telling me that Grandad and I were still one. Then the rope slackened, and he was truly dead.

The Minister read from a book. John Jennings passed round a tray of sand, and we each took some and dropped it onto the coffin. The sand fell, my last words to Grandad, a pattering on the brass plate of the lid.

The Minister got into his car and left.

As soon as our backs were to the grave the hipflasks were out and the men broke into laughter, passing the flasks from one to the other, and voices were raised, with jokes and laughter, all the way to the cars.

At the house, we walked up the path from the gate in silence. The women were waiting with the last libation: fruit cake, cold ham, tea.

And so we buried the triple smith; white, black and lock.

Envoi

In silence of the wind and birds
And wisdom of the fox's bark.
Not clack and cavil of the crowd
Or corpse-light of the pinging screen,
But ancient room of simple words
And embers of the day that's been
And wisdom of the fox's bark
And silence of the wind and birds.

Finis